Conducting Original Research for Your Library

To be a librarian is not to be neutral, or passive, or waiting for a question. It is to be a radical positive change agent within your community.
—R. David Lankes

Conducting Original Research for Your Library

Caitlin Gerrity and Scott Lanning

BLOOMSBURY LIBRARIES UNLIMITED
NEW YORK • LONDON • OXFORD • NEW DELHI • SYDNEY

BLOOMSBURY LIBRARIES UNLIMITED
Bloomsbury Publishing Inc
1385 Broadway, New York, NY 10018, USA
50 Bedford Square, London, WC1B 3DP, UK
29 Earlsfort Terrace, Dublin 2, Ireland

BLOOMSBURY, BLOOMSBURY LIBRARIES UNLIMITED and the Diana logo are trademarks of
Bloomsbury Publishing Plc

First published in the United States of America 2024
Copyright © Caitlin Gerrity and Scott Lanning, 2024

Cover image: Ruslan Kholyaev/Dreamstime.com

All rights reserved. No part of this publication may be reproduced or transmitted
in any form or by any means, electronic or mechanical, including photocopying,
recording, or any information storage or retrieval system, without prior
permission in writing from the publishers.

Bloomsbury Publishing Inc does not have any control over, or responsibility for,
any third-party websites referred to or in this book. All internet addresses given in
this book were correct at the time of going to press. The author and publisher regret
any inconvenience caused if addresses have changed or sites have ceased to exist,
but can accept no responsibility for any such changes.

Library of Congress Cataloging-in-Publication Data
Names: Gerrity, Caitlin, author. | Lanning, Scott, author. Title: Conducting original research for your
library / Caitlin Gerrity and Scott Lanning.
Description: New York : Bloomsbury Libraries Unlimited, 2024. |
Includes bibliographical references and index.
Identifiers: LCCN 2023026528 (print) | LCCN 2023026529 (ebook) |
ISBN 9781440880216 (paperback) | ISBN 9781440880223 (ebook) |
ISBN 9798216171041 (epub)
Subjects: LCSH: Library science–Research–Methodology.
Classification: LCC Z669.7 G47 2024 (print) | LCC Z669.7 (ebook) | DDC 020.72/1–dc23
LC record available at https://lccn.loc.gov/2023026528
LC ebook record available at https://lccn.loc.gov/2023026529

ISBN: PB: 978-1-4408-8021-6
ePDF: 978-1-4408-8022-3
eBook: 979-8-2161-7104-1

Typeset by Newgen KnowledgeWorks Pvt. Ltd., Chennai, India

To find out more about our authors and books visit www.bloomsbury.com
and sign up for our newsletters.

For my boys, Elliott and Oliver. I'll love you forever.
—C. G.
For my wife Maria. I couldn't do this without you.
—S. L.

Contents

1 The Importance of Conducting Research 1

    Essential Questions 1
    Introduction 1
    Original Research 2
    Why Conduct Original Research as a Librarian? 3
    Summary and Reflection 6
    Implementation 6
    Vocabulary 6
    References 7

2 Identifying a Research Problem and Finding Background Information 9

    Essential Questions 9
    Introduction 9
    Scholarship as Conversation 9
    Developing a Research Question 11
    Searching to Learn 11
    Determining an Appropriate Scope 13
    Finding Background Information 14
    Conducting a Search for Information 15
    Summary and Reflection 21
    Implementation 21
    Vocabulary 21
    References 22

3 Writing a Literature Review and Managing Your Information Sources 23

    Essential Questions 23
    Introduction 23
    Writing a Literature Review 24
    Managing Your Information Sources 27
    Summary and Reflection 30

Implementation 32
Vocabulary 32
References 32

4 Research Methods 33

Essential Questions 33
Introduction 33
Conducting Research 33
Types of Research 36
Research Methods 41
Conducting Research Ethically 47
Summary and Reflection 49
Implementation 50
Vocabulary 50
References 51

5 Gathering Data and Descriptive Statistics 53

Essential Questions 53
Introduction 53
Your Library Data 54
Other Sources of Library Data 58
Your Research Data 64
Creating a Data Management Plan 65
Sharing Your Data 67
Descriptive Statistics 68
Summary and Reflection 74
Implementation 75
Vocabulary 75
References 76

6 Statistical Significance, Effect Size, and Power 79

Essential Questions 79
Introduction 79
Statistics 80
Terminology of Statistics 81
Concerns for Generalizability of Research 88
Summary and Reflection 90
Implementation 91

Vocabulary 91
References 92

7 Running and Interpreting Statistical Tests in jamovi 95

Essential Questions 95
Introduction 95
A Brief Overview of Statistical Software 96
jamovi Basics 97
Inferential Statistics with jamovi 98
Summary and Reflection 123
Implementation 123
Vocabulary 123
References 124

8 Sharing Your Research with Others 127

Essential Questions 127
Introduction 127
Evaluation and Transfer 128
Sharing Your Message with Stakeholders 128
Contributing to the Field 129
Summary and Reflection 133
Implementation 133
Vocabulary 133
References 133

9 Putting It All Together 137

Essential Questions 137
Introduction 137
Conducting Original Research for Your Library 137
Implementation 140

Index 141

1 The Importance of Conducting Research

> **Essential Questions**
>
> Use these questions to guide your reading:
> - Why is original research important to the field of librarianship?
> - What research questions am I interested in answering?

Introduction

As two fellow working librarians, we understand the demands on your time. Whether you are in a school, academic, or public library setting, your day-to-day likely consists of prioritizing what must be done to best address your patrons' needs, fulfill your mission statement, or respond to pressing issues by pivoting to a new plan entirely. In many of the facets of the important work that demands our time and attention, library professionals find a need for gathering information, analyzing data, interpreting statistics, and communicating findings, or in other words, conducting original research. While it may feel tempting to think of conducting research as one more thing to add to your already full plate, it can actually be conducted in tandem with your existing workload, while ensuring the myriad of decisions we need to make in the profession are informed ones.

The need for this research can present itself strategically; as a known end-of-year report to stakeholders, or it can present itself in an emergency; as budget cuts threatening library programming or other various needs to advocate swiftly. There is a myriad of other reasons librarians may seek out this text; from continuing education to professional goals and even the desire to engage deeply in the research process we more often teach than practice. Whatever brings you here, you are in good company. Between them, the authors have worked in public, school, and academic libraries, and in each of these settings, they've experienced the need to helm research studies and, in brushing up on their own research skills, wished a text like this one existed.

The Master of Library Information Science (MLIS) is the terminal degree for our field (ACRL 2018). Extensive education and experience in research methods is far more typical of PhD and other doctorate programs, and yet, school, public, and academic librarians with an MLIS often need to engage in this type of rigorous research to support and advocate for their libraries, meet tenure requirements, or participate in publication efforts (Luo 2011; Matusiak and Bright 2020). Librarians need quick and reliable answers to problem-solve in the workplace. This book is intended to facilitate the important work being done in libraries every day. It is designed as an introductory guide and reference book with short, to-the-point information that you can refer to at any stage of a research project. Beyond just "how-to," it will help you choose an appropriate research method to best fit your unique needs. It can help you design and execute an entire research project or serve as a reference manual to answer specific point-of-need questions.

This book will cover the research process, from identifying a research problem to gathering and organizing information, and sharing your findings. It will also focus on specific research methods and provide an accessible overview of statistics as well as strategies for gathering, running, and interpreting statistical measures. Wherever you find yourself in the process, we hope this text will aid your efforts to conduct original library research for the unique needs your community serves. If you aren't sure where to begin, this book can help. Whether you need to formalize your research methods for a dissertation or are looking for something more accessible to the everyday practitioner, this text will provide the information you need to walk through the research process step by step.

Original Research

Conducting research can indicate many approaches to finding an evidence-backed answer to a question. In this text, we will cover the process of conducting original or primary research. Original research is considered a primary source, as it involves designing and conducting a study or experiment to generate and report on the results. In the common vernacular, "doing research" often refers to secondary research, or a person gleaning answers from research they did not themselves conduct. Secondary research is a common approach when seeking the answer to a question that has already been answered by others. For example, there is consensus in the field of library and information science that school librarians have the largest impact on their school communities when collaborating and co-teaching to infuse information literacy instruction across the curriculum. We can find multiple existing studies that confirm these findings. When we reference *original research* throughout this text, the focus goes beyond searching the existing scholarly literature for answers to undertaking a research study from start to finish. Original research involves creating a hypothesis, selecting a research method, gathering and analyzing data, and communicating your results. Primary or original research builds upon the existing body of knowledge to create new knowledge, whereas secondary research references facts that have been established by other researchers. Other theories assert that original research may also consist of interpreting, analyzing, or synthesizing existing research (Ream et al. 2015; Gordon 2007).

Why Conduct Original Research as a Librarian?

Perhaps by now you've identified where this text can support you and are ready to forge ahead. Still others may be asking why librarians should engage in original research? After all, we're expertly trained in the art of information retrieval. Is it not enough to simply find the research that supports our needs in the existing literature? While this may suffice in some circumstances, there are many in which it does not. An episode of ABC's *Shark Tank* (2016) comes to mind. In this show, budding entrepreneurs present their business idea or product to a panel of potential investors and try to convince them to fund their idea. In this particular episode, the investors were not impressed by the candidate's proposal. When asked for proof that his product was effective, he referenced his "evidence pamphlet" (a "works cited" page, one can only imagine). "Read the evidence!" he suggests. One particularly ornery investor exasperatedly retorts, "None of it is *your* evidence!" Another investor agrees, undermining the ask further, saying, "This isn't based on anything you've done. Where are your studies? You should be doing clinical trials!" Clearly the request was not successful. Although this is an exaggerated example, let's pause a moment and apply these principles to the challenging work in which we so often find ourselves engaged in libraries: convincing stakeholders to support an ask or vying for funding. Though different in their patron profiles, funding sources, and budget processes, librarians of school, academic, and public libraries alike have to present their case in the hopes of receiving more funding either for basic maintenance of current services or a special project to serve their communities. Like this budding entrepreneur, making your case effectively can make or break your bottom line.

Advocacy

Advocating for our libraries is often no easy task. This statement is not meant to position libraries as the perpetual underfunded underdog. One needs only to sit through an education or community budget request meeting once to realize that many of the requests competing for funding with the library are also worthwhile ventures that would benefit our communities greatly. The challenge is not only to express what has been discovered within our field already but also to explore it at our local levels and translate our findings into language that our stakeholders value. Oftentimes, evidence from the local level is much more effective than a literature review or works cited we expertly compiled (Goertzen 2017).

In this scenario, let's say the library wants ongoing funding for an Open Educational Resources (OER) position to support the library community in these endeavors. We can easily point to the various existing studies to demonstrate the important impact this type of service can provide, but these results by other researchers may seem nebulous to our stakeholders. Are the results applicable to our population, institution size, and other unique demographics? Each decision-maker likely has their own priorities in mind as they make these allocations—presenting your own research ensures that you are aligned with those and able to communicate the need in a way that speaks directly to their values. In the case of our own library, the authors saw successful funding for OER initiatives once the impact of the program was documented, analyzed, and presented at our own institution and communicated in terms of the broader university's priorities: student retention (Johnson 2016; Liljenquist and Strosser 2022). The ask could have pointed broadly to the "evidence pamphlet" of others who have found benefits through OER initiatives, but it was the savings generated for *our* student population that engaged the administration, brought collaborators on board, and allowed the funding request to be heard in spite of many other worthy, competing requests.

The Dearth of Causal Research

In all areas of librarianship, there is a dearth of causal research, meaning that the relationship between the variables has actually been proven; x causes y, rather than merely x is related to y. You are likely familiar with the common example of flawed correlational research that with increased ice cream consumption comes more shark bites. The relationship is merely the summer months, rather than ice cream consumption causing shark bites. This lack of strong, causal research puts our field at a disadvantage when it comes to advocacy and beyond. Over a decade ago, The American Association of School Librarians (AASL) employed an educational consulting firm to assess the current state of the research connecting certified school librarians and learner achievement (AASL 2021). The resulting report indicated a lack of causal research that the field is seeking to mitigate through strategic research projects such as Causality: School Libraries and Student Success (CLASS). A similar lack of empirical research has been documented related to public libraries as well (Joanna 2008; Sorensen 2021). No matter your specialty in the library world, there's a need that can be filled with high-quality research.

Becoming More Effective Practitioners

Engaging in original research can also help librarians stay engaged in the practices we so commonly teach to others. Our degree programs and work experience prepare us to be experts at information retrieval and, in our various roles, we are accustomed to adeptly walking users through pieces, if not the entirety, of the research process. However, immersing ourselves in the process of conducting such research gives us a fresh and meaningful perspective to bring back to our patrons and our practice.

Still others may be motivated to conduct research to advance not only the field of librarianship but also their careers. Whether you find yourself on the tenure-track, intend to pursue an advanced degree, or enjoy the networking and collaboration opportunities that come from scholarship, conducting your own original research is a way to step into the important conversations happening in our field, expand your professional learning community, and exercise your passion for libraries.

So why should you do research? To help you make data-driven decisions based on the best evidence available to improve library functions and services. This is known as evidence-based librarianship (EBL). In order to practice EBL, to make good decisions based on evidence, there needs to be a body of evidence that librarians have discovered through research (Eldrege 2000; Crumley and Koufogiannakis 2002). We conduct research to answer those questions we have about our services and programs, to improve our libraries, to build a knowledge base for our discipline, and to benefit the whole profession. It gives us the opportunity to work with colleagues both within and outside our libraries, to work with researchers, to obtain grant money, to improve the visibility of our libraries, and to advance our careers.

Summary and Reflection

In this chapter we discussed just some of the reasons that might drive librarians to conduct their own original research in service of our libraries and patrons; there are countless more that may have brought you to this text. In the following chapters, we will review the stages of and strategies for conducting original research. Rather than awaiting research from others occurring in settings that may not match our own, conducting original research empowers practitioners to step into that role and answer their own workplace questions in a systematic, reflective, and data-driven manner. This approach arms us with the local data we need to convince our stakeholders, inform our own practice, and implement informed changes in our libraries. What is your motivation for engaging in the original research process? Clarifying your research mission is an important first step in the process. Whether you are taking a data-driven approach to library leadership, practicing what you teach, growing your career, or something else entirely, this text will provide you with the support you need to be successful.

Implementation

Think about some broad topics that are relevant to your unique original research needs. Create a mind map of potential subtopics and avenues for you to explore. Do some initial searching in a library database or Google Scholar and reflect on the following questions: Which have already been answered in the literature? Which are the most interesting or relevant to you moving forward?

Vocabulary

- Action research
- Casual research
- Evidence-based librarianship
- Original research
- Primary research
- Secondary research

References

American Association of School Librarians. 2021. *Educational Research Applied to the Shared Foundations: A Report of the CLASS II Research Project*. American Library Association. https://www.ala.org/aasl/sites/ala.org.aasl/files/content/advocacy/research/docs/AASL_ClassIIResearch_Book.pdf.

Association of College and Research Libraries. 2018. "Statement on the Terminal Professional Degree for Academic Librarians." Guidelines, Standards, and Frameworks. American Library Association. April. https://www.ala.org/acrl/standards/statementterminal.

Crumley, Ellen, and Denise Koufogiannakis. 2002. "Developing Evidence-Based Librarianship: Practical Steps for Implementation." *Health Information & Libraries Journal* 19, no. 2: 61–70.

Eldredge, Jonathan D. 2000. "Evidence-Based Librarianship: An Overview." *Bulletin of the Medical Library Association* 88, no. 4: 289.

Goertzen, Melissa J. 2017. "Introduction to Quantitative Research and Data." *Library Technology Reports* 53, no. 4: 12–18.

Gordon, Mordechai. 2007. "What Makes Interdisciplinary Research Original? Integrative Scholarship Reconsidered." *Oxford Review of Education* 33, no. 2: 195–209.

Joanna SIN, Sei-Ching. 2008. "Disparities in Public Libraries' Service Levels Based on Neighborhood Income and Urbanization Levels: A Nationwide Study." *Proceedings of the American Society for Information Science and Technology* 45, no. 1: 1–15.

Liljenquist, Rosie, and Charla Strosser. 2022. "All the Better to Teach You With: Integrating Academic Composition, Information Literacy, Fairy Tales, and OER." In *Intersections of OER and Information Literacy*, edited by Mary Ann Cullen and Elizabeth Dill, Chicago: ACRL.

Luo, Lili. 2011. "Fusing Research into Practice: The Role of Research Methods Education." *Library & Information Science Research* 33, no. 3: 191–201.

Matusiak, Krystyna K., and Kawanna Bright. 2020. "Teaching Research Methods in Master's-Level LIS Programs: The United States Perspective." *Journal of Education for Library and Information Science* 61, no. 3: 357–82.

Otto, Jane Johnson. 2016. "A Resonant Message: Aligning Scholar Values and Open Access Objectives in OA Policy Outreach to Faculty and Graduate Students." *Journal of Librarianship and Scholarly Communication* 4: eP2152.

Ream, Todd C., John M. Braxton, Ernest L. Boyer, and Drew Moser. 2015. *Scholarship Reconsidered: Priorities of the Professoriate*. John Wiley & Sons.

Shark Tank. 2016. Season #7, episode #29, aired May 20, on ABC.

Sørensen, Kristian Møhler. 2021. "Where's the Value? The Worth of Public Libraries: A Systematic Review of Findings, Methods and Research Gaps." *Library & Information Science Research* 43, no. 1: 101067.

2 Identifying a Research Problem and Finding Background Information

> **Essential Questions**
>
> Use these questions to guide your reading:
> - How can I determine an appropriate topic for my research project?
> - What strategies can I employ to begin to build my knowledge around this topic?
> - What are some effective ways to search for information on my chosen topic?

Introduction

The previous chapter discussed the importance of conducting research for your library as well as the advantages of bringing original research results to your stakeholders or decision-makers. Practitioners engaged in the day-to-day operations of library spaces and services likely did not find it difficult to brainstorm a short list of pressing issues that need to be addressed. But how do we decide what is worthy of being addressed via a more formalized research process? This chapter will focus on the intertwined, initial stages of research: determining your research question and conducting a search for information.

Scholarship as Conversation

Libraries were founded on the concept of sharing knowledge and information for the betterment of society. In its "Core Values" the American Library

Association (ALA) describes the contributions of libraries as "support for efforts to help inform and educate the people of the United States" (ALA 2019). Public libraries are at the forefront of this work in our communities and their professional organization calls for engagement in research as part of its strategic plan. The Public Library Association (PLA) strives to "measure [its] impact on the library field in order to adapt to new trends and models" (PLA 2022). In all areas of librarianship, data-driven processes are valued as we seek to serve our communities and act as stewards of public funding through well-informed best practices.

The Association of College and Research Libraries (ACRL) has a Framework for Information Literacy for Higher Education. One of those frames is "Scholarship as Conversation." Essentially, the meaning of this frame is that the research landscape is a conversation beckoning you to participate. In this way, we are interacting with our peers who are wrestling with similar questions and building a collective body of knowledge. Even if you consider yourself to be a novice researcher, your initial stages of inquiry invite you to enter this conversation. We see this in a more concretely way at professional conferences in our field. There, a spectrum of researchers from novice to the foremost can be found discussing their findings and we can engage in conversation with them during the Q&A section of their presentations or other networking events. Our work in libraries can sometimes feel isolating, especially if you work in a small library as a department of one. The landscape of scholarship teaches us that we are not alone and there are many others are wrestling with similar issues in libraries across the country and even the world. By entering this conversation, we create a community of like-minded scholars who share, uplift, and inspire future research.

There are similar values reflected in the best practices for school librarians. The American Association of School Librarians (AASL) National School Library Standards emphasize practices such as inquiry, collaboration, and engagement that mirror the concept of "scholarship as conversation" by engaging with an "interconnected global learning community" (AASL 2018, 114). In the AASL Standards Framework for School Librarians, the charge is for librarians to empower students to not only "seek knowledge" but also "create new knowledge," (AASL 2018, School Librarian, I.D.3) "cultivate networks" (AASL 2018, School Librarian, III.B.3), and guide "the dissemination of new knowledge" (AASL 2018, School Librarian, VI.C.2). As quoted in the AASL National School Library Standards, "example isn't another way to teach, it is the only way to teach" (Hermanns 1983). School and academic librarians are encouraged to model these best practices for their students.

Developing a Research Question

To find a topic, you can examine the projects you are working on and see if they have the potential to be used for research. You can take note of any issues that may arise in your library as a potential source for research. You can talk to your colleagues about their projects and problems. You can also read the literature and read the calls for programs at upcoming conferences to get a feel for the kinds of research topics that are in demand.

Once you have a topic, you need to develop a research question. In general, it should have three parts and be precisely and clearly stated as it will guide your research. Your question should have a what, a who, and an outcome. The "what" is the thing or new thing you want to evaluate. The "who" are the people that interact with the "what." The outcome is the effect that the "what" had on the "who." In simpler terms, you try a new summer reading program, and you want to determine if the children in the program experienced an increase in their desire to read. The "what" is the new summer reading program. The "who" is the children in the program. The outcome is the change in their desire to read. Your research question becomes: How did the new summer reading program affect the children's desire to read?

A more formal approach to building a good research question, and by extension a good hypothesis, is the PICO approach that comes from clinical research. PICO stands for *population*, the group or people you are going to study; *intervention*, the program or treatment to which the population will be exposed; *comparison intervention*, the standard intervention or control that you will use with another group if you are using a control group; and *outcome*, the impact or effect that the intervention had on your population (Crumley and Koufogiannakis 2002, 63).

Searching to Learn

At this stage in the research process, you should begin to take your brainstorming a step further by combing through the literature to see what directions other researchers have taken with similar issues. Identifying similar studies can help you narrow your list of questions because some may have already been answered. However, keep in mind that the body of knowledge in the field grows stronger as replication studies confirm similar findings (Oakleaf and Kyrillidou 2016). The studies related to your topic may also inspire interesting new research paths for you to pursue. In the "future research" section of scholarly articles we get to read the researchers' thoughts about what gaps still exist even after their efforts. The questions these researchers feel still need to be answered can be informative and inspiring to our own research. These can be a great jumping-off point and a way to contribute meaningfully to the field.

Entering the scholarly conversation can happen quite informally from behind your computer screen. One only has to open a library database related to their field and conduct a preliminary search on their topic to begin to engage with these researchers and their respective work. This scan of the research landscape helps us build familiarity with the avenues and subtopics already being explored in our area of interest and is a helpful way to begin to focus our own research question.

The work of gathering background information on your topic of choice is very closely intertwined with the material we will cover in the next chapter on conducting your literature review. Searching for articles on our topic and subsequently using those search results to narrow or broaden our focus are very interrelated tasks. Because of this interrelated nature, we will discuss searching for information in this chapter as well. It is important to remember that research is a cyclical process where we are free to move forward and backward between the different stages, rather than a linear process where we must choose a topic and then begin our search without ever revising or rethinking our original idea.

Consider the Reflective Inquiry Model (Figure 2.1) for a visual representation of the research process. Note that the directional arrows between each stage go forward and backward, indicating that movement through the stages does not need to be linear (Lanning and Gerrity 2022).

The brainstorming, or thinking, stage is an important one on its own. The initial topics you consider for your own research will be the jumping-off point for your initial searches. Because your chosen research focus is so intertwined with preliminary searching, I recommend exploring the databases near the beginning of this process so that searching and refining are happening at once. This process of allowing your search results to inform the narrowing or broadening of your topic is called "Searching to Learn" (Diekema and Haderlie 2013). Within any broad topic area, there are many offshoots and subtopics to explore. You want your research question to be focused enough that it is suitable for your given capacity and parameters. Some of the questions you need to answer to help establish an appropriate scope are as follows:

- How many people will be working on this research project?
- What type of resources do we have to put toward this research?
- What is our budget for this project (if any?)

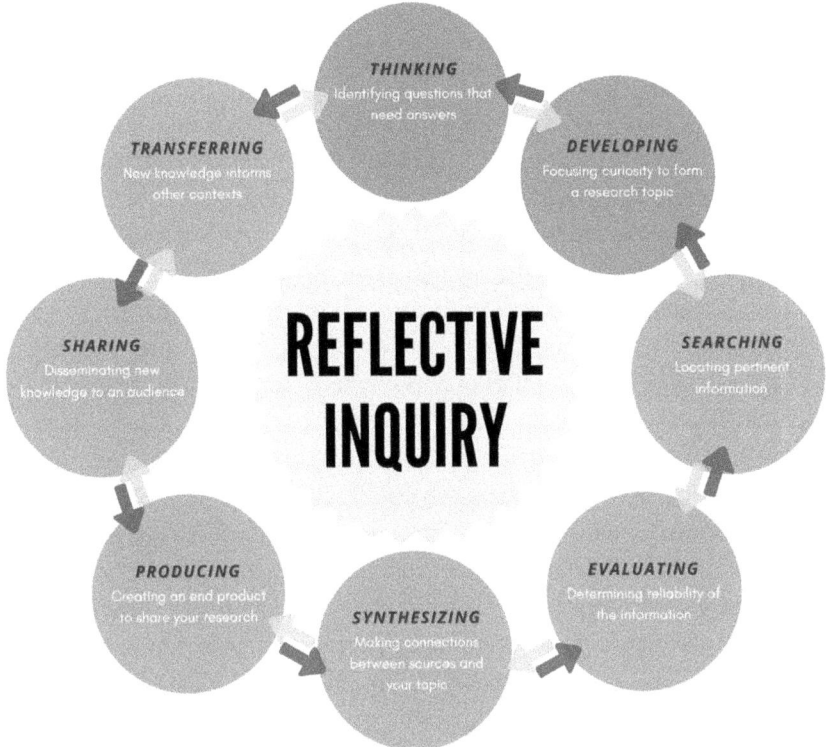

Figure 2.1 *Reflective Inquiry Model.*
Source: Authors.

Answering those initial questions will help you begin to determine how large of a scope or ambitious a project you can undertake. An academic librarian at an R1 institution with access to a research lab and research time built into their schedule can pursue a much more ambitious scope than a librarian at a smaller institution where research is an added bonus rather than a work requirement.

Determining an Appropriate Scope

Still, regardless of the size of your institution, consider inviting colleagues to collaborate with you. It's worth thinking about your ideal type of collaborator. It can be rewarding to work with others toward a shared research agenda. By partnering with those who complement your own strengths and weaknesses, you can accomplish more. If you find yourself to be a goal-oriented and organized individual, perhaps you will be drawn to collaborate with big-picture thinkers who can dream up a project and keep you inspired, while you keep the project on a focused timeline. Perhaps one researcher will have more strength in statistical methods while another is a stronger writer. Define these roles, set regular meeting times, and establish an agreed-upon goal that you can work towards together.

Perhaps your timeline will be driven by an institutional need, such as annual budget requests. Another idea to set the pace of your research is to think about where you might share your results more broadly with the library community. Is there a conference related to your library niche or specialty that you'd like to submit a proposal to and perhaps present at their next conference? If so, take a look at the next deadline for proposals. Set your research agenda around those opportunities. Oftentimes, the themes of these conferences can be another helpful way to focus your research project. What is the emphasis of the national organization for this year and how can you fit your question into that theme? Other important considerations that can help shape your research agenda are thinking about approval through your institutional review board, if relevant.

Ultimately, there are no hard-and-fast rules for determining your research topic, only strategies to guide you toward a topic that is relevant and a scope that is manageable. These will vary by person, topic, institution, and resources.

Finding Background Information

Gathering background information is an important step before trying to dive headfirst into the formal literature review stage and should not be skipped. This stage can not only help you further refine your topic but also allow you to define any unknown concepts or terminology and give you a broader understanding of the research landscape surrounding your topic. Some good starting places for gathering background information on a topic are:

- Encyclopedias and reference books
- Introductory chapters to books on the broader topic
- Wikis, blogs, and other less formal sources
- Magazine articles or presentations from your respective professional organization

Building familiarity through less formal information resources will help you grow your understanding of the topic more broadly, identify and define unfamiliar jargon, and ease you into the conversation at an accessible place. Just because we wouldn't cite a Wikipedia article on our topic doesn't mean it's a bad place to start growing our understanding of a topic. The next section will cover strategies to gather more formal information resources—the kind we can and will cite—but don't discount the importance of building your knowledge base from informal sources!

Conducting a Search for Information

Anyone outside of direct patron instruction in information literacy skills may find a refresher in our own best practices to be helpful. If this is the stuff of your daily work, you may find you could have written this section yourself. Read on if a reminder of information retrieval skills would be useful to you!

Selecting a Database

Choosing where to search will depend on your institutional access. Those working in academic libraries likely have great familiarity and even a preferred scholarly database to conduct their searches. Colleagues in public and school libraries may need to rely upon a more limited selection depending on funding and availability in your locality. If your institution has limited access to these sometimes-expensive subscription research databases, a good alternative is often your respective state-funded digital library. To locate these online library resources in your state, a search for your state name and "digital library e-resources" should help. You may need to contact your State Library or local public librarian for an access code or login, but these resources are provided free of charge to residents within that state. Some examples are Utah's Online School Library (https://onlinelibrary.uen.org/), South Carolina's Virtual Library (https://scdiscus.org/), Pennsylvania's Electronic Library (https://powerlibrary.org/), and the online resources available through California's State Library (https://www.library.ca.gov/services/online-resources/).

Some of the more popular subscription databases specific to Library and Information Science research are:

- LISA: Library and Information Science Abstracts
- LISTA: Library, Information Science, and Technology Abstracts
- Library Literature and Information Science Full-Text

However, access to these will likely only be provided through larger academic libraries. Multidisciplinary as well as education databases are another good avenue to explore:

- Academic Search Premier or Ultimate
- Academic OneFile
- Education Full-Text
- Subscriptions to database collections listed under the platform provider such as EBSCO or GALE

Other free scholarly databases are provided through the government or open-access resources:

- ERIC: Education Resources Information Center
- DOAJ: Directory of Open Access Journals
- ScienceDirect
- SpringerOpen

Lastly, Google Scholar is an option for surveying the scholarly landscape on a subject; keeping in mind the "library links" setting to route you around paywalls will save time and frustration where full-text access is concerned. Google Scholar can be a great way to find and access many of the open or government-provided literature as well.

Advanced Search Techniques

For those who would benefit from a refresher in advanced search settings, this section will focus on Boolean operators, limiters, and other advanced search techniques to make your database searches most effective.

Boolean Operators

The three most commonly used Boolean operators are

- AND
- OR
- NOT

AND will combine two separate ideas, instructing the database to return you with results that have both terms or phrases present. AND will narrow your search. A simple AND statement such as *makerspaces AND library* will ensure that

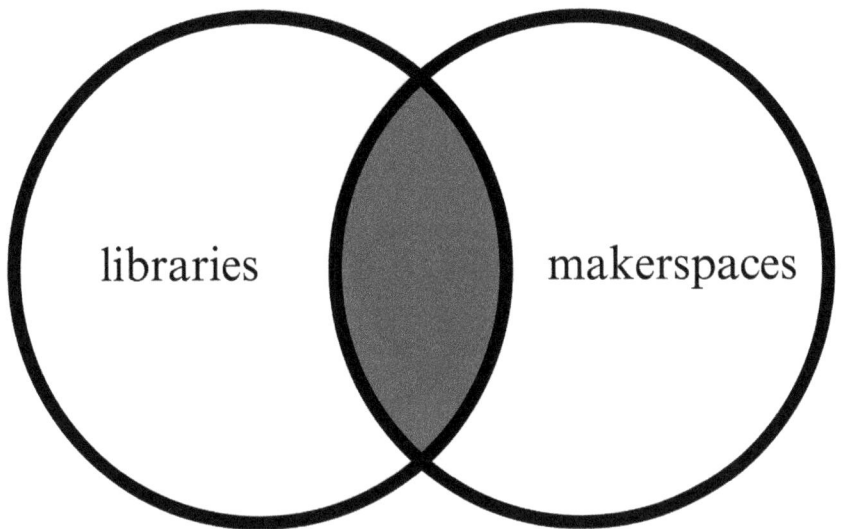

Figure 2.2 *Boolean operator "AND."*
Source: Authors.

the database is only retrieving articles where makerspaces are discussed in the context of a library rather than a different setting (Figure 2.2).

OR is the most useful Boolean operator for accessing synonyms or adjacent terminology, giving the database flexibility around the terminology you've selected, which will broaden your search to bring back more results. It is important to remember that search terms linked with OR must be nested in parentheses as part of your search strategy. Like the order of operations in a math equation, the database reads these operators and search strategies like an algorithm. Using OR without parentheses can confuse the search engine and explode your search in unhelpful ways.

Consider the search statement:

makerspaces AND library AND (school OR K12)

The additional AND focuses our search further by adding another concept. The use of OR provides some flexibility. We can see that this researcher is looking for articles on makerspaces in libraries in a school setting but is using OR for flexibility around how this is expressed by the scholars (Figure 2.3).

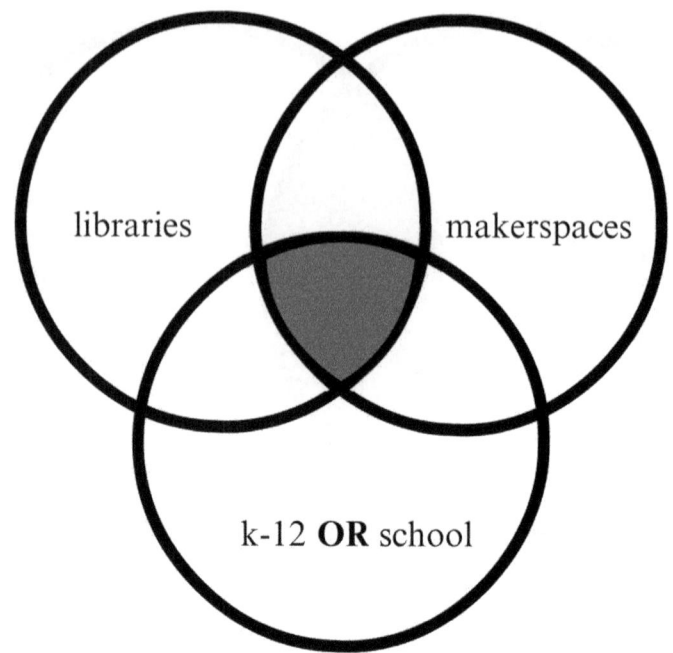

libraries **AND** makerspaces **AND** (k-12 **OR** school)

Figure 2.3 *Boolean operator "OR."*
Source: Authors.

Lastly, the Boolean operator NOT can be used to eliminate results that you are certain you do not want. This is helpful when you want to eliminate a term from your search entirely. Use this operator judiciously, as it will limit your results, but it can be useful in certain situations. For instance, if you were searching for examples of makerspaces in libraries and did not want results from the K-12 sector, you could use the search statement (Figure 2.4):

makerspaces AND libraries NOT (school or K-12) to eliminate those results.

Limiters or Facets

When our search brings back many results, we can limit by publication date, source type, language, and many other criteria. Perhaps we want to tell the database

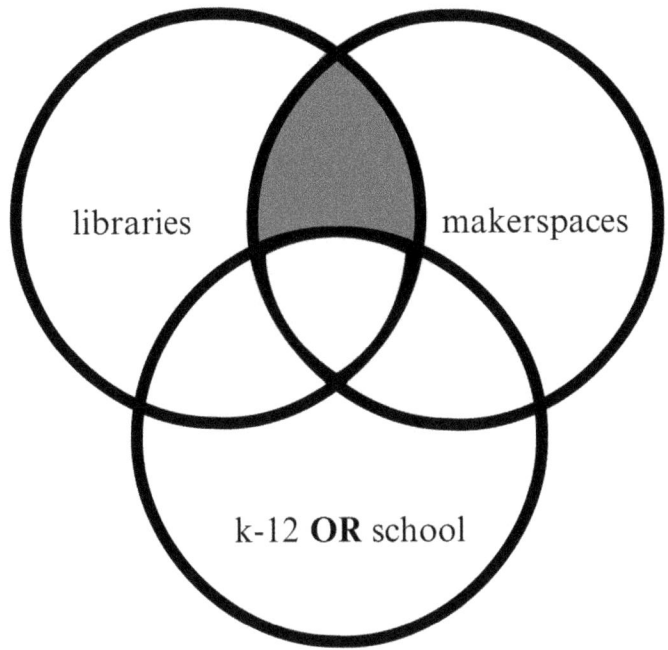

Figure 2.4 *Boolean operator "NOT."*
Source: Authors.

to only bring back peer-reviewed results that have been published in the past decade. The options, often in a separate menu in the margins of the database, allow you to further narrow your results without adding additional search terms (Figure 2.5).

Other Advanced Search Techniques

Using an asterisk for truncation will allow the database to search for alternative suffixes after the root of a word. For instance, athlet* will bring back results with the search term alternatives: athlete, athletes, athletics, athleticism. These should be used cautiously, as truncating some words may bring back unrelated terms. Consider the following example: truncating the word illness at ill* will bring back illogical, illusion, and even Illinois. To encourage the database to find alternatives for illness, the OR operator is a better option: (illness OR sickness OR disease).

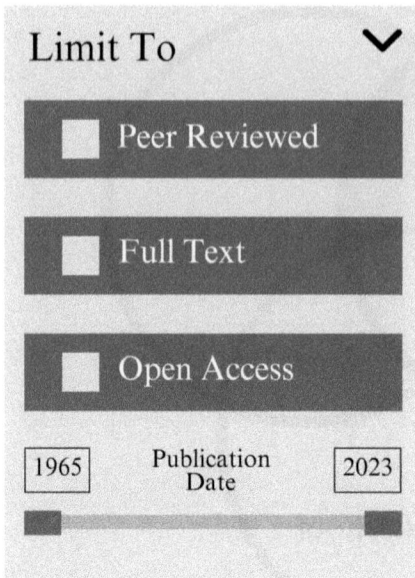

Figure 2.5 *Limiters.*
Source: Authors.

The phrase operator is simply quotation marks placed around a phrase you'd like to search in that exact order. The search: *community service AND libraries* would be well served by adding quotation marks around the phrase "community service" because, individually, those words can mean so much else. Without the phrase operators, the database effectively searches for those words anywhere in the article. So, you could get results about libraries being described as a great service to the community, which does not quite have the same meaning as "community service." With the phrase operator, it is up to you to determine how important the keywords are to be kept together in your results as a phrase. The search for *"therapy animals" AND libraries* will bring back results on exactly that specific type of animal. Without the phrase operator, we risk clouding our results with articles that list a number of disparate activities occurring in a library: from wildlife encounters with animal ambassadors to bibliotherapy sessions.

Interlibrary Loan

We will save the discussion on information equity for another book but suffice it to say that gaining free access to high-quality, peer-reviewed information resources can certainly be challenging depending on the information access privileges afforded to you by your institutional affiliation. If your institution has a limited budget for access to these subscription resources, interlibrary loan will be an invaluable resource for your research endeavors.

Summary and Reflection

This chapter highlighted the early stages of the research process that form the foundation for your work moving forward. Research is a process that begins well before any data is collected. There is an idea that needs to be developed, background research to be done, and a research question that needs to be generated to guide the process. While it is worthwhile to spend time brainstorming about your research questions, the sooner you begin to combine your brainstorming process with searching the professional literature, the better. Taking part in the scholarly conversation helps you to operate less in a vacuum and rely upon the body of knowledge already being shared in our field. Which of your questions have already been answered and what new directions were you inspired to explore?

Replication studies can be valuable in generating local data for your own institution. Will you pursue an unexplored area or design a replication study of your specific library? Take the time to search for, access, and engage with the resources surrounding your intended topic before moving on to the next chapter.

Implementation

Write a research question using PICO. Create an effective Boolean search statement and use the "Searching to Learn" technique to further refine your research question. Choose some resources to begin engaging with and initiate interlibrary loan requests for any information sources that you need help accessing.

Vocabulary

Boolean operator
Database
Facets
Interlibrary loan

Limiters
Nesting
Peer-review
Phrase operator
Scope
Truncation

References

American Association of School Librarians (AASL). 2018. *National School Library Standards for Learners, School Librarians, and School Libraries.* Chicago: ALA.

American Library Association (ALA). 2019. "Core Values of Librarianship." https://www.ala.org/advocacy/intfreedom/corevalues.

Crumley, Ellen, and Denise Koufogiannakis. 2002. "Developing Evidence-Based Librarianship: Practical Steps for Implementation." *Health Information & Libraries Journal* 19, no. 2: 61–70.

Diekama, Anne R., and Haderlie, Sheri. 2013. "Searching to Learn: Using Search Results to Build Concept Knowledge." *Instructional Technology and Learning Sciences Faculty Publications.* https://digitalcommons.usu.edu/itls_facpub/253. Accessed January 14, 2023.

Hermanns, William, and Albert Einstein. 1983. *Einstein and the Poet: In Search of the Cosmic Man.* Brookline Village, MA: Branden.

Lanning, Scott, and Caitlin Gerrity. 2022. *Concise Guide to Information Literacy.* Santa Barbara: Libraries Unlimited.

Oakleaf, Megan, and Martha Kyrillidou. 2016. "Revisiting the Academic Library Value Research Agenda: An Opportunity to Shape the Future." *Journal of Academic Librarianship* 42, no. 6: 757–64.

Public Library Association (PLA). 2022. "PLA Strategic Plan 2022–2026." *American Library Association.* https://www.ala.org/pla/about/mission/strategicplan.

3 Writing a Literature Review and Managing Your Information Sources

> **Essential Questions**
>
> Use these questions to guide your reading:
> - To which scholarly conversation is your research contributing?
> - How can we situate our research meaningfully for our audience?
> - What are some strategies for writing an effective literature review?
> - How can using a reference manager and synthesis matrix help organize our information resources?

Introduction

The previous chapter discussed how to identify a research topic and effectively search the literature, which can be done in tandem to most effectively establish a scope for your project. As you delve into the literature and become more familiar with the prominent issues, authors, and philosophies around your chosen topic, formalizing the existing information resources into a literature review is often the next step in the research process. We will also introduce useful strategies for managing, organizing, and citing your information sources.

Writing a Literature Review

Whether your research will be shared formally or informally, a thorough literature review will serve you well. As you seek answers to your questions, a good place to start is in the existing body of published research (often referred to as "the literature") where others have shared their progress along similar lines of questioning. This can include scholarly articles, books, conference proceedings and presentations, media, and more. Whether the results of your research will be submitted for publication, presented at a conference, or informally shared among your colleagues, a literature review ensures that you aren't missing out on high-quality information—strides that others in your field have already made toward solving similar problems. Having a thorough grasp of these scholarly conversations will increase your understanding of broader interrelated concepts and strengthen the credibility of your own work. Performing a literature review also ensures that your question has not already been answered by others, saving you valuable time. It is essential as it not only informs your own research process, but also helps us to credit those whose work came before, lending legitimacy to your approaches. A literature review can inspire new directions for your research endeavors as you identify gaps—or understudied areas— in the field.

The field of library and information science is part of the larger umbrella of the social sciences, where literature reviews are typically synthesized to include an analysis of closely related sources as they inform the topic at hand. A literature review will establish the context of your intended research for your audience. It will overview any frameworks or theories, and clarify the scope of your research by pointing to the seminal work as well as emerging studies that comprise the current state of knowledge surrounding your topic. It is important to note that a literature review ought to feature your voice—a critical analysis rather than a rote summary. Think of this exercise in critical thinking as the stage that will set an important foundation of understanding for your audience and form the broader context and the purpose of your research—important aspects to establish before moving forward. The literature review tells a story that should include where and how your research fits into the big picture (Fink 2019). Questions we may consider throughout the process of conducting a literature review include:

- What is the scope of my research?
- Am I striking a good balance of thoroughly examining my question without getting pulled into too many subtopics?
- Do I have the most up-to-date research as well as seminal work?

- Will this help my audience better understand the topic?
- Have I found contrary points of view, not just those that are in line with the way I see things?
- Am I critically analyzing the issue rather than simply summarizing?
- Do I need to make any changes to the focus of my project?

Scholarship as Conversation

The ACRL frame "scholarship as conversation" is a helpful way to discuss the importance of a literature review (ACRL). When you are conducting research, you are entering the conversation among scholars in your field. The process of finding, retrieving, and analyzing the existing body of research can be likened to joining a networking event at a professional conference—the work and writings of everyone from the most cited researchers to novice graduate students are intermingled, overlapping, and striving to move the field forward with interesting discoveries, new directions, and probing questions. By identifying gaps in the literature, you can attempt to establish your place in the web of existing knowledge or conduct a replication study among your own unique settings and demographics to confirm existing findings. This chapter seeks to provide a framework for conducting a literature review in the field of library and information science and managing the resulting influx of information.

Conducting a Literature Review

Preparing a literature review begins with an effective search in the places where you are most likely to uncover the current research in the field. Having access to library databases such as Library and Information Science Abstracts (LISA) or a broader multidisciplinary library or education database is ideal, though Google Scholar works as well. If you aren't provided access to these subscription databases through your school or workplace, try the public library or state library website where you live. You want access to high-quality, peer-reviewed literature, so you'll need to avoid your favorite search engine because these resources often live behind a paywall. Google Scholar may prompt you to pay for these articles, so utilize your local library to access these subscription resources. You can link Google Scholar to your preferred library in the settings to make retrieving the articles you find easier. You'll need to verify your membership to the library, and then Google Scholar will link you directly to the resource behind that organization's paywall. You'll also want to search for books on your topic in your preferred library's catalog or using a site like worldcat.org.

You will also need to construct an effective search statement using terminology related to your research topic, carefully linking the words and phrases with Boolean operators and using the facets to limit your search results by publication date, source type, and the like. This process is covered in more depth in the previous chapter. Once you've narrowed your search, it's time to select the resources that most closely address your topic. Remember to carve out time to request these articles if they need to be borrowed through interlibrary loan. Research is a time-consuming but worthwhile process!

The next step is to immerse yourself in the literature to become a mini expert on this topic. Read, read, and read some more. Take notes to refer back to and follow the trail of other researchers and studies you'll undoubtedly uncover as you dive into the literature. As you engage deeply with the research, you'll start to identify patterns: the key researchers and landmark studies that always seem to be cited; if you haven't read them, track them down! This is a constant process of discovery, engagement, and yes, reading. While highlighting all of the interesting progress and findings surrounding your topic, be sure to also include any gaps you've identified, controversies, or areas where the research conflicts. Be careful to avoid "cherry-picking" sources that support your line of questioning and include the full picture, even if it challenges your thesis.

A common question at this stage is, "How do I know when I'm finished?" This stage can indeed feel overwhelming. Information overload is real. Because research topics overlap, there will always be a new avenue to follow, so keep your scope in mind and read as deeply as will inform your research topic. You'll eventually find that the sources all begin to point to each other—meaning you aren't uncovering more studies as you progress through the sources you've found—and you can begin to feel confident that you've done your due diligence.

Writing Tips

When writing your literature review, you'll want to avoid excessive quoting. Reserve quotations for particularly salient excerpts that are not better served through paraphrasing. Be sure to include your own voice and analysis that focuses on the evidence that was established in the sources you found. It can be helpful to review examples of other literature reviews to inspire your process. You'll encounter plenty of examples as you read through the research articles you find. This advice is not to encourage copying another author's style, but rather, to get you into the headspace of scholarly writing. Much like reading Shakespeare, you might feel rusty at first, but the more time you spend immersed in the specialized language, the more familiar the process will feel. Imagine your audience as you write: what information do they need to better understand your intended research?

Managing Your Information Sources

Reference Managers

At this point of the process, it can begin to feel—much like your internet browser—that your brain has too many tabs open! You likely have found many helpful articles that cover different aspects of your research topic, and it can be hard to keep track of it all. Luckily, there are many free reference management programs to help you stay organized: Zotero, EndNote, and Mendeley to name a few. These tools allow you to save your research, organize it, and, even help you cite it correctly with time-saving plug-ins that connect your gathered sources to your word processor. Setting up one of these reference managers may take more time up-front but will pay dividends when it comes time to generate your works cited.

These reference managers work to save your research as you find it, so there is no need to re-create that perfect search each time. You can organize your research into folders however you choose: by project, by topic, and so on. These tools are free to use and operate on your desktop and in the cloud to access your research wherever you are. They have citation plug-ins for your word processor and can automatically cite your research with a few clicks of your mouse in many different citation styles. When undertaking a research project, a reference manager is a highly recommended tool for organizing and citing your sources.

Citation Chaining

Another way to ensure your literature review as thorough as possible is to use citation chaining. Citation tracing or chaining can be done both backward and forward. Backward citation chaining means finding other promising research in the sources you've already discovered. You can discover them throughout the reading (in the literature review section in particular) or scan the bibliography for other potential sources (Figure 3.1) (Seattle University Library 2017).

Forward chaining means using citation tools—like those available in Google Scholar—to see where the article you've discovered has been cited. You can look for links such as "cited by" to see all of the articles that have cited that particular source (Figure 3.2).

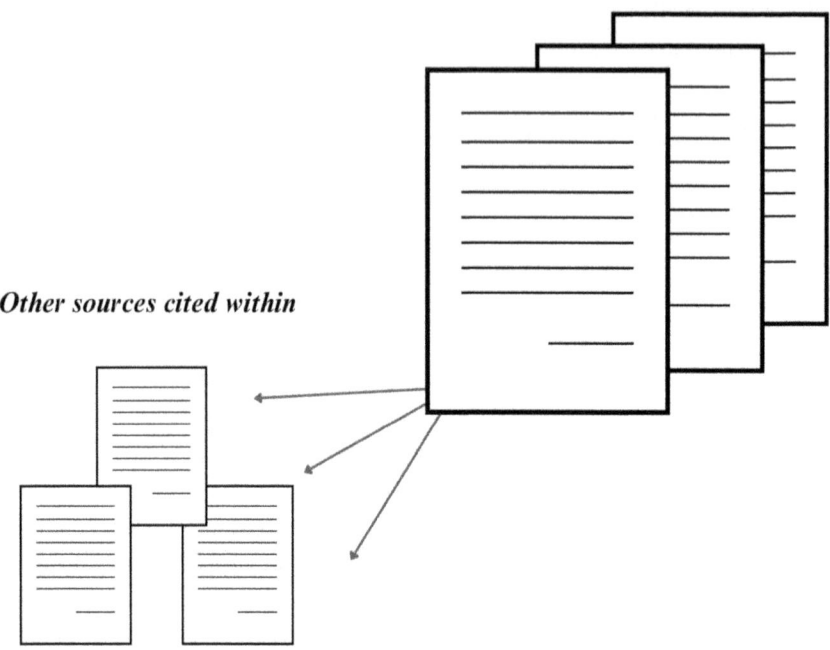

Figure 3.1 *Backward citation chaining.*
Source: Authors.

Forward and backward citation chaining can help assure you that your literature review has been thorough, as you'll either find new, related sources, sources outside of your scope, or the same sources you've already discovered in your previous search. Once you begin to see the same articles again and again, you can feel confident that your search has been thorough. You can also use notification settings to be alerted when a new work cites one that is central to your research to make sure you are capturing the most current research.

Synthesis

While reference managers can help you save, cite, and even notate your research, they can't help you with the actual writing of the literature review. This is where a synthesis matrix comes in handy. While a synthesis matrix may sound intimidating, it's just a simple table that can facilitate connection-making across your sources. It can be tempting to write a literature review by reporting source by source, however, that is neither interesting nor useful to your reader and is in

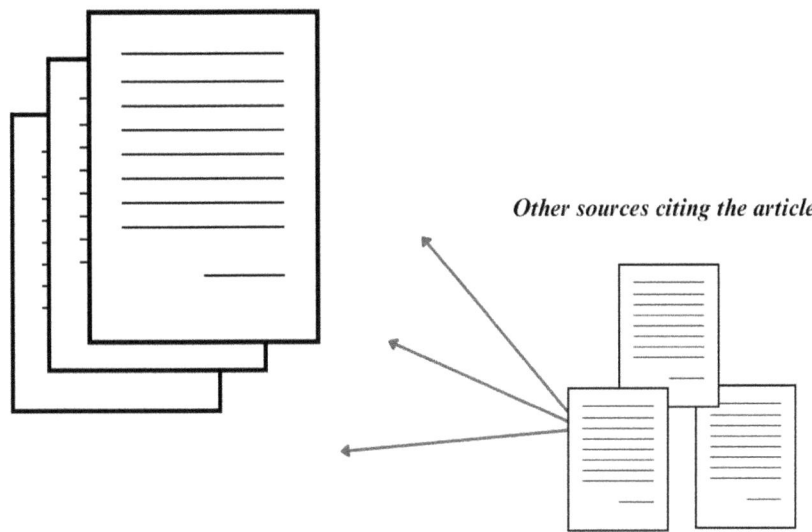

Figure 3.2 *Forward citation chaining.*
Source: Authors.

fact closer in function to an annotated bibliography than a true literature review. One of the key responsibilities you have as the author of this literature review is to make connections between the individual sources, to highlight the meaning as they relate to your topic (Lundstrom et al. 2015). An effective literature review goes beyond a source-by-source summary akin to an annotated bibliography. The literature review tells the story, extracts the meaning, and summarizes the key findings as they relate to the questions posed by your research. It lays a foundation for a reader who is less familiar than you, pays homage to the relevant researchers who have come before, and answers the question of what we already know and what we're still striving to discover. It gives your research a purpose and a context.

To create a synthesis matrix, first create a simple table (Table 3.1). You can sketch this by hand or create it in a spreadsheet. Each column is a source, and each row is a main idea or topic.

You'll fill in the cells where the topic is represented in each source. As the matrix is developed, it becomes an outline for your eventual end product, where each row could serve as a subtopic. In this way, your writing becomes thematic, highlighting interesting connections between the sources and leaving plenty of room for your own interpretation of how this relates to your larger topic and research project. How you record information in the cells is up to you: a summary

Table 3.1 *Synthesis Matrix Template*

Research Question:					
	Source #1	Source #2	Source #3	Source #4	Source #5
Main idea #1					
Main idea #2					
Main idea #3					
Main idea #4					
Main idea #5					
Main idea #6					

Source: Authors.

of what you'd like to share or a salient quote. Paraphrase carefully while using the synthesis matrix and always indicate if something is a direct quote. You do not want to accidentally plagiarize when revisiting your matrix throughout your writing process. Notice in Table 3.2 that each cell is not filled in—this is to be expected, as not every article will discuss the same subtopics.

Summary and Reflection

This chapter discusses the management of the information sources that will inform your research. From conducting a literature review to synthesizing and managing information sources, there is much to read and organize in the process of conducting original research. To which scholarly conversations do you hope to contribute through conducting original research? Who are the key researchers in the field surrounding your research question?

Conducting a thorough literature review to explore the conversations around your research topic will empower you to appropriately credit and build upon the work of others in the field. Does your research endeavor require an informal or formal literature review?

There are tools to help you manage all of the information resources you will encounter in this process. Reference managers are useful tools for saving, organizing, and citing your sources. Which reference manager will you try? Finally, a synthesis matrix can help when it comes time to make sense of it all. Do you have any other tools in your writing toolbox to make integrating information resources into your research project easier?

Table 3.2 Synthesis Matrix Example

Research Question:
What are the ethical concerns of integrating artificial intelligence (AI) tools into library services?

	Kaushal, V., and R. Yadav. 2022. "The Role of Chatbots in Academic Libraries: An Experience-based Perspective." *Journal of the Australian Library & Information Association* 71, no. 3: 215–32.	Brown, L. M. 2022. "Gendered Artificial Intelligence in Libraries: Opportunities to Deconstruct Sexism and Gender Binarism." *Journal of Library Administration* 62, no. 1: 19–30.	Gasparini, A., and H, Kautonen. 2022. "Understanding Artificial Intelligence in Research Libraries: An Extensive Literature Review." *Liber Quarterly: The Journal of European Research Libraries* 32, no. 1: 1–36.	Cox, A. 2022. "The Ethics of AI for Information Professionals: Eight Scenarios." *Journal of the Australian Library and Information Association* 71, no. 3: 201–14.
Patron Privacy	Respondents' perceived risk of privacy intrusion was high. Encryption should be considered for use of chatbots in libraries to build users' trust around sharing personal data.		"Libraries should understand the power they hold over their customers and critically reflect on their use of data analysis technologies." (p. 18).	AI is dependent on use and storage of user data and this lack of privacy can cause hesitation or avoidance among prospective users.
Gender and Sexism		Digital assistants/voice assistants tend to be typecast as women, reinforcing traditional societal gender roles.		"It is not surprising that AI is biased when women, people of color, people with disabilities and older people are under-represented among those designing it" (p. 13).
Bias			One solution is to host AI laboratories to introduce patrons to this new technology (including potential bias in the algorithm).	Algorithm bias is inherent and perpetuated based on historical inequities being reproduced.

Source: Authors.

Implementation

Select a reference manager and set up an account to make organizing and citing your research easier as you engage in the research process.

Vocabulary

> Boolean operator
> Citation chaining
> Endnote
> Literature review
> Mendeley
> Paywall
> Reference manager
> Synthesis
> Sources
> Zotero

References

Fink, Arlene. 2019. *Conducting Research Literature Reviews: From the Internet to Paper*. Thousand Oaks, CA: Sage.

Lundstrom, Kacy, Anne R. Diekema, Heather Leary, Sheri Haderlie, and Wendy Holliday. 2015. "Teaching and Learning Information Synthesis: An Intervention and Rubric Based Assessment." *Communications in Information Literacy* 9, no. 1: 4.

Seattle University Library2017. Citation Chaining with Google Scholar [Video File]. June 30. https://youtu.be/idGkqlj1Emg.

4 Research Methods

> **Essential Questions**
>
> Use these questions to guide your reading:
> - What is the scientific method?
> - What research methods are there?
> - How can I conduct my research ethically?

Introduction

In Chapters 2 and 3 we discussed "scholarship as conversation"—the idea that your research has the power to move the field forward by contributing to the existing body of literature. It is time to start thinking about undertaking your own research project and adding to the scholarly conversation. In this chapter, we present an overview of what research is and why it is important for you, as a library professional, to conduct it. Then we will briefly describe various research methods and end with a discussion of research ethics.

Conducting Research

The Scientific Method

The scientific method is an approach to conducting research, beginning with a question that needs an answer. We formulate a hypothesis to test, collect data, analyze it, and report our findings that either confirm or refute our hypothesis. The *Oxford English Dictionary* defines research as "systematic investigation or inquiry aimed at contributing to knowledge of a theory, topic, etc., by careful consideration, observation, or study of a subject" ("Research" 2022). The *McGraw-Hill Dictionary* of *Scientific and Technical Terms* defines the scientific method as the "systematic collection and classification of data and, usually, the formulation and testing of hypotheses based on the data" (2003). The ideas of the scientific method and research are very similar, which shows how ingrained the scientific method is in our understanding of the research process. If we combine these two definitions, we have our working definition of research using the scientific method, which is the systematic investigation through collection, classifications, and analyses of data in order to test hypotheses and contribute to knowledge and theory in a discipline or field.

Not all library professionals conduct formalized original research, for a variety of reasons related to their job description and demands, interest, resources, and more. However, any library professional can be empowered to undertake this process. Library professionals conduct informal research on the job all the time, for instance, when analyzing reference desk usage to adjust staffing or looking at circulations by subject to adjust collection development decisions. Formalizing the process does involve complex tasks. Picking a topic to research is not trivial. Statistical analyses involve high levels of mathematical skills. Synthesizing results into a report requires higher-order thinking skills, and the publication process can be daunting. However, there is easy-to-use software that can complete the statistical analyses for us, and our libraries can be an inspiring source of ideas for research topics. We attempt to demystify the process in this text and provide helpful guidance. Read on to learn more about research methods and ethics.

Defining Research

The United States Department of Health and Human Services defines research as "a systematic investigation, including research development, testing, and evaluation, designed to develop or contribute to generalizable knowledge" (Office for Human Research Protections 2017). Another definition of research, this time from a scientific dictionary, says that research is a "scientific investigation aimed at discovering and applying new facts, techniques, and natural laws" ("Research" 2003). These two definitions help illustrate the two broad categories of research: basic and applied.

Basic research is also known as pure or theoretical research, and it is designed to advance knowledge as is mentioned in the first definition. Applied research is designed to solve real-world problems and corresponds to applying facts and the discovery of techniques mentioned in the second definition. It is important to know that these categories are not mutually exclusive. Your research can contribute to the general knowledge of librarianship while solving a problem within your library.

Research may also be viewed from another perspective as either inductive or deductive. Inductive research looks to infer patterns and theories through the collection of observational data. Deductive research starts with a theory and aims to support or disprove it with the collection of data. Inductive research moves from the specific, the observations, to the general, a theory that explains the observations. Deductive research moves from the general, the theory, to the specific, collection of data to test the theory.

Bhattacherjee states that "inductive research is also called theory-building research, and deductive research is theory-testing research" (2012, 3). When you start to think about your research, you need to consider if your research will build theory or apply it. Will it add to the librarianship knowledge base, or will it solve a problem, or will it be some combination of the preceding?

Hypothesis

Research is guided by a hypothesis. A hypothesis is a statement of what the researcher believes they will find as a result of their study, experiment, or research when they examine the relationship between two or more variables, elements, or factors. Statisticians use the term variable to represent the values to be examined. An example hypothesis could be as follows: The new summer reading program will affect children's desire to read. This hypothesis is non-directional. It does not indicate whether we believe that our reading program will have a positive (or negative) impact on the desire to read. We can change our hypothesis so that it becomes a directional hypothesis: The new summer reading program will increase children's desire to read. Now we are stating that we think the reading program will have a positive impact on the children in the program.

Here is another example. A library tries displaying books with the cover out and believes that there was an increase in circulation of those titles. They decide to collect data to see if that is really the case. They formulate a hypothesis: books displayed with their covers facing out have higher circulation rates than books that are displayed with their spines out. The hypothesis is an assumption they make. They believe it to be true. They will test this assumption to see if it is accurate. They pick fifty titles from their collection and examine how many times they circulated in the past three months. That data forms one of the variables. Then they display those same fifty titles with the covers facing out and collect circulation data for three more months. That is the second variable. Each title in each set will have its own number of circulations. In other words, the values are variable.

To determine whether the assumption in the hypothesis is true, a null hypothesis is developed. This is the first confusing thing we will encounter when working with statistical testing. The null hypothesis is the opposite of what we want to prove to be true. The null hypothesis for our example would be that books displayed with their covers facing out do not have higher circulation rates than books displayed with their spines out. The null hypothesis is denoted as H_0. Our original hypothesis, what we want to prove, is called the alternative hypothesis and is denoted as H_1 or H_a. Then we test the null hypothesis. We use the null hypothesis because it can be tested through statistical analysis. Statisticians do not say that we have proven the null hypothesis to be false. Instead, they say that the analysis shows the null hypothesis is statistically unlikely to occur by chance, and therefore it is probable that the differences found are the result of the influence of one variable upon another.

Types of Research

We are often presented with research as binary, opposed choices. There is basic research. Then there is applied research. It is experimental research or nonexperimental research. It is quantitative research versus qualitative research. However, this is not the case. There is a lot of overlap. When you are reading through the descriptions below, keep that in mind.

When we first consider doing research to solve a problem or investigate the effectiveness of a program, we do not start by saying, "I want to do a basic, quantitative, quasi-experimental research project." We start by examining the issue and thinking about what kinds of information we need to collect in order to see the outcome. Then we think about how we will design the research process so that we can do it given our resources and how we will gather the information we need. The design and the information we want to collect will determine the type of research we will be doing.

Basic

Basic and applied research are two broad categories of research. Basic research or pure research is undertaken to expand our knowledge and to prove theories. It does not try to solve a problem. It tries to advance our understanding of a phenomenon, and it does not concern itself with application.

Applied

Applied research looks to solve problems. It is research undertaken to find solutions or a better way to build or do something to improve outcomes. Basic and applied research are not mutually exclusive. You can look to solve a problem while also expanding the knowledge base of our discipline and supporting or proving a theory.

Action Research

Action research can be viewed as a specific type of applied research. It is a potential avenue for conducting original research that can help us more quickly address an issue in our library while also applying principles of data collection and critical reflection. Action research has its own cyclical process that does not necessarily involve running statistical tests. It is designed to solve a specific issue or problem with a practical solution. It does not seek to provide generalizable knowledge, but it may help others who find themselves with similar problems in similar contexts. Often employed by the social sciences, including the field of education, action research is an empowering, systematic research method that speaks to the busy and demanding roles in librarianship. If you find yourself questioning when you'll ever find time to conduct research, action research may be your answer. If you are regularly making decisions in your library, action research formalizes that process.

Kemmis and McTaggert, as illustrated by Stubeck, outline the process of action research as follows: reflect, plan, act, observe, reflect, then plan, act, observe, and reflect as necessary (2015, 31). First, a problem is identified and researched. A plan is developed to address the problem, then action is taken. The results are evaluated, and a modified plan is developed to improve upon the previous outcomes. Once again, action is taken and the results are observed. Stringer, as mentioned by Smith, boils action research down to three steps: look, think, and act (2017). Then repeat as necessary. Rather than waiting for the final, published conclusion to act, the action research model encourages the researcher to intervene or act, not in a vacuum, but as part of the process. Reflection ensures that iterations and improvements can be made as more is learned.

Experimental

Experimental design involves the random assignment of people to either experimental or control groups. The experimental group receives the treatment or program that is being studied. The control group gets a placebo or the old program. A pre-test and post-test may be used to determine if groups improved and by how much. There can be more than one experimental group to test multiple new treatments or programs. Experimental designs allow researchers to look closely at the effect of a specific treatment on a specific population. Experimental designs test for cause-and-effect relationships. Population is a new term. A population is every member of the group of interest to be studied. This could be second graders or public library cardholders who are sixty-five years of age or older. The number of people in the population is represented by N. You may have $N = 1,000$ library card holders aged sixty-five and up, for example. You want each of the control and experimental groups to look similar, to be representative of the population you are studying. In other words, you would not compare the results of a reading program if the experimental group was all high-achieving students and the control group was all low-achieving students. A true experimental design can be difficult to implement because of the requirement for random assignment. Random assignment means that test subjects are placed into either the control or experiments by chance.

Quasi-experimental

A quasi-experimental design is the same as an experimental design without random assignment. For example, if you wanted to evaluate the effectiveness of your library instruction on eighth graders at your school, and your school has three classes of eighth graders, you would not take them out of their classes and form new groups. Instead, you would randomly assign one class as the control group and the other two classes as the experimental group. If one of those classes was for high-achieving students, you would exclude them from the experiment and use only the two classes that more closely resembled each other assigning one to control and the other to experimental groups. Even though the classes are randomly assigned, the individuals in them are not; this makes the design quasi-experimental. Any design where you have to use non-random assignment for some reason is quasi-experimental.

Nonexperimental

Nonexperimental methods do not use treatments. There is no experimental or control group. This is a very broad category of research. It embraces many different research methods. It includes qualitative methods like case studies and observational studies, and it includes quantitative methods like regression analysis and correlation studies.

Qualitative

Qualitative research collects attitudes, opinions, and beliefs of the subjects being studied in a systematic manner in order to understand "qualities, or the essential nature, of a phenomenon within a particular context" (Brantlinger et al. 2005, 195). It describes what happened, unlike quantitative research, which captures numeric data. Qualitative data or information often takes the form of text as the subjects state their thoughts on the questions asked. Analyzing text can be time-consuming and involved. You may need to train others to help you code and classify the information you collected. There is software that can help you analyze text-based information, including R packages. R is an open-source software that is used for statistical analysis. R packages are add-ons that extend R's basic functionality. We will mention a little more about R in Chapter 7. It is important to understand your role in interpreting the data. Can you be objective? Do you intend to interpret the information through a specific lens or point of view? How did your presence influence the information you collected?

Qualitative research is sometimes described as inductive, moving from the specific to the general. You observe a class of freshmen at your institution performing a research task. From this very specific context, you develop generalizations and theories about how students perform research. This theory can then be tested in a quantitative study. However, qualitative research can also be deductive. It can move from the general to the specific. You can start with a theory of how students conduct research, and move to the specific, documenting how they actually did research and whether their approach supports your theory.

A number of the research methods listed below are qualitative methods. However, this book will focus on quantitative methods in the next three chapters. There are many sources where you can further explore qualitative research. *The Sage Encyclopedia of Qualitative Research Methods* is one example.

Quantitative

Quantitative research methods are a structured and systematic investigation of numerical information or changes in measurable numeric data of the population of interest. It strives to create generalizable results that describe a phenomenon or the effect of an intervention, treatment, or program. It deals with things that can be counted, measured, and used in mathematical formulas. Test scores are an example, as are door counts, circulations, and attendance at programs.

Quantitative research is often what we think of first when we envision research projects. We see numbers and formulas and might feel overwhelmed, intimidated, or confused. We may believe that we cannot do that kind of research, but this book exists to show you that you can. Quantitative research is not the only kind of research, but it will be the focus of the remainder of this book.

Quantitative research requires an alternative hypothesis and a null hypothesis. Data is collected and analyzed for a sample that represents the population being investigated. The results of the analysis are found to be either significant or not, and tables are often presented that show the results of the analysis. Conclusions are drawn based on the size and generalizability of the effect of the treatment on the subjects of the study.

Measurement Scales

Quantitative research classifies the data it uses into four categories called measurement scales. They are nominal, ordinal, interval, and ratio scales.

Nominal scale data is categorical data that has no implied order. One answer is not any better than another. You may collect data on what breed of dog people own. It does not matter whether poodle or pug is checked. There is no right answer, and one breed of dog is not better than another. You can count nominal data and give percentages. You can look at which answer was given the most often. This is known as the mode.

Ordinal scale data is like nominal in that it is also categorical data, but there is an order or ranking to the information. For example, you may ask your patrons to rank their satisfaction with their recent interlibrary loan experience. You provide a five-point scale of ranked choices moving from extremely satisfied to extremely unsatisfied. There is no way to measure levels of satisfaction on a standardized scale. The step from neutral to satisfied and from satisfied to very satisfied will be different for each person who answers the question, but there is a ranked order to the choices. This order makes that data ordinal. In addition to the basic math mentioned for nominal data, ordinal data allows you to find the median, the number in an ordered set of values such that half the answers have higher values and half have lower values. There are a few special statistical tests that can be used with ordinal data. Categorical data can be either nominal or ordinal in nature and is another way to refer to these types of data. This can get confusing. It may help to remember that textual data is categorical data. Whether that data has no order or is ordered determines if it is nominal or ordinal.

Interval scale data builds on ordinal data. They have a meaningful order and, additionally, there is a consistent and measurable distance between values. The difference between 45 and 46 is the same as the distance between 51 and 52. Temperature measured in degrees Fahrenheit or Celsius are examples of interval scale. You can find the mean and standard deviation with interval data, and many statistical tests are now available to be used.

Ratio scale data adds one thing to the interval scale, a true, absolute 0 value. To use the temperature example, the Kelvin scale has an absolute value of 0, representing the total lack of temperature. Ratio data can be the number of books in your collection expressed as an integer (10,000) or the average number of reference questions received on a Tuesday (54.367) expressed as a rational number. All kinds of math and statistical tests can be used to analyze ratio data. Interval and ratio data combine to form continuous scale data. Where textual data is categorical data, numeric data will be continuous data with the absence or presence of a meaningful zero value determining whether the data is interval or ratio in nature.

Mixed Methods

Mixed methods research combines both qualitative and quantitative research methods. Surveys often have questions that collect data and ask for opinions or feelings. This is an example of mixed methods. The idea is to leverage the strengths of each approach and get a more detailed and holistic picture of the phenomenon being studied.

A good mixed methods project does not use its qualitative and quantitative data separately but integrates their use. The Harvard Catalyst website lists three basic mixed methods research designs that illustrate the integration. The first one is Convergent Parallel Design. In this design, qualitative and quantitative data are both collected and analyzed, then the results are compared and related to each other, and finally interpreted and discussed. The other two designs are sequential, starting with one method and then moving to the other to further the results ("Mixed Methods Research" 2022). Using a mixed methods design may give your research more credibility because the results of each method confirm the other's findings.

Research Methods

The research methods listed below were generated from a number of sources. It is not comprehensive. It serves as an introduction to the various methods that can be used in library research. The list was developed by consulting articles that investigated the most popular research methods used in published library research (Chu and Ke 2017, 288; Togia and Malliari 2017, 53), specialized encyclopedias (Salkind 2010; Mills, Durepos, and Wiebe 2010; Given 2008), articles about research methods for librarianship and related disciplines (Crumley and Koufogiannakis 2002, 66; Eldredge 2004; Brantlinger et al. 2005, 197), and a professional organization (American Library Association 2022).

Action Research. Action research is usually a qualitative method undertaken to solve a specific problem through an iterative process.

Bibliometrics. Bibliometrics is a quantitative study of publication information. Citation analysis is a form of bibliometrics. It collects data on the number of times an article is cited and where the cited information appears. The information can be used to determine important and influential articles or journals in a field.

Case Study. A case study is a qualitative analysis commonly used in business. It is an in-depth study of a business or library to understand the how and why of their success or failure. It can be used to examine a specific process. Case study research involves observations, interviews, and life histories. While a case study is tied to a specific organization at a particular time, the intent is to uncover generalizable principles and/or practices that lead to success or failure.

Causal Comparative. Also known as ex post facto, causal comparative studies look for changes in behavior or outcomes that have already occurred due to a treatment or intervention. This type of study is less precise because the researcher has little control over outside factors that could have influenced the results. It is easier to implement but may be best used as a preliminary investigation.

Content Analysis. This qualitative method involves examining the words and concepts used in documents to understand the messages that are being imparted in an objectively fashion.

Correlation. This method uses quantitative data to look for relationships among variables. Relationships can be positive or negative. For a positive correlation, as one thing increases so does the other. In a negative correlation, as one thing decreases, the other increases, and vice versa. We can use correlation studies to show that library usage has a positive effect on grades. However, it is important not to confuse correlation with causation. Library use may indicate that students using the library are studying more than students who do not. It does not necessarily mean that they are using library databases, or getting research help from a librarian.

Ethnography. This qualitative method seeks to describe or interpret a group of people and their culture. It can use observation, interviews, and content analysis.

Factorial Designs. This quantitative method examines the effects of more than one treatment or intervention on participants. It allows research to examine how well the treatments work together and individually. If you had three instructors teach information literacy using two different approaches, you would have a 3 × 2 factorial design. The notation has two digits, the 3 and the 2. This indicates that you have two variables or treatments that you are examining. The first variable, the 3, indicates that there are three levels or categories to this variable corresponding to the three different instructors. The second variable has two levels that represent the two approaches to instruction. This can be an economical way of examining multiple variables, but you may need to recruit a large number of participants to fill out the necessary groups.

Focus Group. A focus group is a qualitative method that involves the interview of a group of people by a moderator to solicit their opinions and feelings about something. For example, you can use a focus group to examine your proposed website redesign. The insights gained from the group's perspective then lead to changes in the website's design. The moderator plays an important role in keeping the group on track and not allowing one person to dominate the group.

Gap Analysis. A gap analysis is a quantitative method that looks at the differences between desired and received levels of service provided by the library. As an example, you can survey people as they ask questions at the reference desk. You ask them what level of service they expected to receive and what level of service they did receive. When you look at the numbers, you find that users of reference expected the help they received to be an 8 out of 10, but they felt they received only a 4 out of 10. That is a large gap. You can then look at comments and identify ways to close the gap and bring expected and received service levels closer together. This can be a difficult method to undertake on your own, especially if you want to look at multiple services at the same time. You can contract with LibQual to provide a standardized survey instrument for you to use to find gaps in service delivery throughout the library, and because it is a standardized, national survey program, you can compare your library to others. You may discover that you are doing things well.

Grounded Theory. In this method, researchers gather information from participants through observation, interviews, or other methods and analyze the information to generate a theory that explains the behavior.

Interpretive Research. This method of qualitative research uses a specific frame or theory to analyze events or documents. For example, you can analyze library services from a capitalist, Marxist, or feminist perspective.

Life History. This qualitative method involves in-depth interviews of people to gather information on their lives in general or specific events from their lives and share their perspectives. Special collections departments in our libraries often collect oral histories that give us a broader understanding of our communities.

Longitudinal or Cohort Study. This research method can be qualitative, quantitative, or mixed. It follows one group of people through time and at designated intervals; information is collected regarding some ability or knowledge they have gained formally or informally. You could test the information literacy knowledge of freshmen and then retest the same group in their sophomore, junior, and senior years to see how their knowledge has improved. You could ask them if they had formal information literacy instruction or not and develop a fuller picture of the levels of skill development over time.

Meta-analysis. A meta-analysis is a quantitative method that combines comparable data from similar studies into one dataset, and then runs statistical tests on the combined data to provide stronger evidence for any outcomes. It can be problematic if the data sets are not closely aligned or if the most appropriate statistical tests are not used.

Narrative Review. The narrative review is a qualitative method that is also called a review article. It is an extensive literature review designed to provide readers with a summary of a specific topic. Many of our libraries have books with titles that start with "Annual Review of…." This is an example of a narrative review that attempts to summarize the latest research in a field.

Pre-experimental Design. This method either eliminates the control group and examines one group after a treatment, or it examines one group with pre- and post-test exams. It could examine two groups, one being a "control" group and the other the experimental, but no pre-test is given, only a post-test is administered after treatment. It is a simple design and assumes any changes are due to the treatment. However, without control groups or pre-test exams, the validity of the tests or strength of the conclusions can be challenged by other possible explanations. This method can be used to quickly see if a larger, more rigorous study of an intervention is warranted.

Pre-test–Post-test Using Intact Groups. This is a quantitative design that is categorized as quasi-experimental, because of the lack of random assignment of participants to control and experimental groups. It is easier to use this method when working with classes of students. For example, you can give new information literacy instruction to one class of eighth graders, the experimental group, and the old information literacy instruction to another similar class of eighth graders, the control group. Each class receives the same pre-test, and then after the instruction, a post-test. The differences between the pre- and post-test scores are analyzed. If there is a significant difference between pre-test results of the two groups, then the results of the post-test cannot be compared. Assuming the classes are very similar, then the post-test results can be compared. If the new instruction leads to a significant improvement, then the control group, the other class of eighth graders, should also receive the new instruction.

Program Evaluation. When we evaluate a program, we frequently use both qualitative and quantitative methods to determine if it was a success. A program evaluation should be done in a systematic manner and generate information that allows the program to be compared to a local or national benchmark. This can involve counting the number of people who attended a program and collecting their opinions about the quality and usefulness of the program, then comparing that number with attendance figures and satisfaction data of other programs.

Randomized Controlled Trial. This is the research method we associate with clinical trials of new drugs or medical procedures. It is a quantitative method that can take three different forms. The pre-test–post-test method is the same as the pre-test–post-test using intact groups mentioned above, but with random assignment of people to the experimental and control groups. Random assignment eliminates the problem of possible differences between intact groups, like a class of students. The next form is post-test only. It is used when a pre-test cannot be given or may influence the outcome of the post-test. Again, people are randomly assigned to control and experimental groups, and one group receives the treatment. Both groups are given a post-test and differences are compared. The ability to accurately calculate the gain is lost without information from a pre-test. The final form is the Solomon four-group design. There is one experimental group and three control groups. The experimental group receives pre-test, treatment, and post-test. The control groups receive different combinations of treatment and pre-test, but all receive the post-test. This is best illustrated in a small table as seen in Table 4.1. This design allows for factorial analysis of pre-test and post-test and provides better generalizability of results.

Research Diary. This qualitative research method asks participants to keep track of how they interact with databases, the research process, and other events or activities. It collects the participants' actions, thoughts, and opinions about the

Table 4.1 *Solomon Four-Group Design*

Group	Pre-test	Treatment	Post-test
Experimental	X	X	X
Control 1			X
Control 2		X	X
Control 3	X		X

Source: Authors.

process being studied. Their diaries are gathered and analyzed to look for patterns and generalizations about behaviors and opinions.

Secondary Data Analysis. This quantitative method takes already existing data and analyzes it. We collect a lot of data in our libraries. We can use that data to help answer questions about our services, or to explore answers to research questions. We will explore this topic in depth in Chapter 5.

Survey. Surveys can be qualitative or quantitative, but often use mixed methods to gather data. It is a very common practice in librarianship, in part because it is both easy and economical to do. It can solicit opinions and collect demographic information. Likert scales, rating something on a scale from very poor to excellent, for example, can be used to quantify opinions. Surveys can be conducted as interviews or online questionnaires. It is important to test your survey questions before releasing your survey. Questions can steer participants to specific answers, have obvious or implied bias, or may not reflect what you really want to know. Trying out your survey on a few colleagues and a few volunteers is a good way to improve the quality of your questions, thereby improving the results you will receive from your survey.

Systematic Review. A systematic review is similar to a narrative review. It reviews and summarizes either qualitative or quantitative research studies using a pre-defined, rigorous, "systematic" method to assess the primary research regarding a specific topic to produce a conclusion about best practices. The methodology minimizes bias that can be part of narrative reviews. It is often used in clinical research. The methods used must be clearly explained and be reproducible. Reproducibility is the ability of one researcher to examine another researcher's study, rerun it, and generate the same results. In libraries, you could examine all the primary research articles on late fees. Using the data gathered from the articles, you would draw a conclusion about the effectiveness of late fees and determine whether you would use them or not.

Transaction Log. Transaction logs are captured by our computer systems and contain information on search terms, databases used, and records viewed. Search terms could be used as both qualitative and quantitative data, while the other information is quantitative. COUNTER 5 statistics obtained from database vendors give us another way to gather this type of transactional usage information. COUNTER statistics include information on database usage and records viewed and downloaded, and because they are collected in a standardized format, the information is comparable across years and libraries. Our websites can yield transactional information through the use of programs like Google Analytics (https://analytics.google.com) or Siteimprove (https://www.siteimprove.com). These systems tell us which pages get the most use and how many clicks it takes to get to them among other things. Transaction information can be used for collection development purposes and to improve our websites.

Unobtrusive Observation. Unobtrusive studies generate qualitative data by carefully observing participant behaviors in particular situations. For example, you can give students a research task, and then watch how they proceed to investigate the topic. You cannot intervene to help them or correct poor search strategies. Data is used to look for patterns and generate theory. The presence of the observer can influence behavior and the lack of interventions could be potentially problematic. Observation is part of many other qualitative research designs. It can be used to observe how well reference librarians are performing at the desk.

Conducting Research Ethically

Research needs to be conducted ethically. When you gather data from various library sources, you need to ensure that the data cannot be traced back to an individual. Our circulation systems can do this for us by telling us how many times a book has been checked out, but not by who. It is important to ensure the privacy or anonymity of our patrons' data.

If you are conducting surveys, observing student behaviors, gathering information from focus groups, or using any data that contains identifying information of individuals or companies, your research needs to follow specific ethical guidelines and be approved by a research board. The approval process ensures that your research checks all the boxes and presents minimal risk to the subjects who participate in the research. Colleges and universities have institutional review boards, or IRBs, that have the authority to approve, disapprove, or require changes to research before it can be conducted. Public schools also have review boards, often at the district level, that approve research conducted with students. Public libraries generally do not have a review board, so you may need to ask a supervisor about getting approval or work with a colleague at a university.

There are three levels of IRB reviews. To get IRB approval at any level, you first fill out the required forms providing all the requested information and follow the submission process. The lowest level is an exempt review. The research proposal for an exempt review presents no more than minimal risk which is defined by the Department of Health and Human Services as "the probability and magnitude of harm or discomfort anticipated in the research are not greater in and of themselves than those ordinarily encountered in daily life or during the performance of routine physical or psychological examinations or tests" (Office for Human Research Protections 2017). Exempt research must fall into one of a few specific categories of research like involving normal educational practices, educational tests, or food taste and quality evaluations. Exempt reviews can be evaluated by one person from the IRB, and often are approved quickly.

The next level of review is an expedited review that also has no more than minimal risk, but the categories of research vary, including clinical drug studies and the collection of blood or biological samples, and also include a broad category of behavioral and survey/interview research. One or two members of an IRB can approve this research. The last category is the full board review. If your research has more than minimal risk or deals with vulnerable populations that include minors, it will need a full board review. This level of review typically takes the longest time.

An important aspect of the approval process is the creation of the informed consent form. Prospective participants deserve to know about the study so that they can give their informed consent to partake. The consent form contains information about the study, what is being studied, how long their participation will take, whether there are any benefits to participating in the study, and how information will be handled regarding confidentiality or anonymity. Additionally, the informed consent form should tell participants that they may leave the study at any time with no consequences. If questions in the study may cause emotional distress, participants need to know that, and the consent form should provide information on where to receive help if a participant is adversely affected by the study. The name of the person conducting the study, called the principal investigator, and their contact information should be included to address any questions that a participant may have. Finally, if the study involves minors, parents must give consent for their children to participate, and the children must assent to participate in the study.

There is a class of research that does not require approval by a review board known as classroom research, which involves conducting research within the scope of your job when you have no intent of sharing the result outside of the organization for which you work. In other words, if you are a teacher, trying new pedagogical methods, examining student results, drawing conclusions about the new pedagogy, and sharing your findings with your fellow teachers at your school is part of what you do. If you are a librarian, collecting the number of questions asked at the reference desk, the type or even specific questions asked, the answers provided, and whether the patron was happy with that answer is within the scope of your work. It is a normal part of the job you do. If you think you might want to present your findings to a larger audience, then you need to seek approval from an IRB.

Be aware that approval takes time. Boards meet on a set schedule, and if there is some aspect of your proposal that they want to be modified, you will have to make changes, send the proposal back, and wait again for their approval. If you work at a university and are working with a colleague in a school or public library, then you may need to get your research proposal approved by both entities. It is very important to plan ahead and look into whether your proposal needs to be approved and by whom. If you are unsure, ask your colleagues and supervisors, find someone who has been through the process, or contact your IRB until you get a satisfactory answer.

Summary and Reflection

In this chapter, we saw that research is important to every field of study. It creates a base of knowledge that the field is built upon. It also provides evidence for best practices and decision-making. In the research process, usually, both the alternative and null hypothesis need to be considered. What obstacles do you need to overcome for you to do a research project? Are there new skills you need to learn, or a colleague you can work with who will bring expertise to the project? How will you schedule your time?

You can use the PICO method that was introduced in Chapter 2 to think about your experiment in terms of the people or groups involved, the intervention you want to try and judge its effectiveness, whether you will use a control group, and what outcome you hope to achieve. As you think about your research, what methods will work best for your research plan? Do you need to gather more information on that method? Is there an expert you can ask about appropriate methods for your research?

It is important to conduct research ethically. You need to think about what and who will be involved in the research. Information in the form of data from a number of library sources generally presents no ethical issues for research. However, research that involves people, even at the level of an anonymous survey, needs special ethical consideration. If you work for an institution that has an IRB, you need to follow their outlined procedure to get your research approved. How will you conduct your research ethically? Is there any potential for harm and how can this be mitigated? Will you be working with minors or adults, and how will you get informed consent? Who do you need to talk to or work with to get your research project approved?

Implementation

Use the research question that you developed earlier to generate an alternative hypothesis, and a corresponding null hypothesis. Examine the list of research methods above and pick two possible research methods that you think would best address your hypothesis. Find the IRB body for your institution and practice filling out the forms. This will help you organize and flesh out your research project.

Vocabulary

Action research
Alternative hypothesis
Applied research
Basic research
Classroom research
Data
Deductive research
Exempt research
Experimental research
Inductive research
Informed consent
Institutional Review Board
Interval scale
Methodology
Mixed methods research
Nominal scale
Nonexperimental research
Null hypothesis
Ordinal scale
PICO
Qualitative research
Quantitative research
Quasi-experimental research
Ratio scale

References

American Library Association. 2022. "Research Methods." LARKS—Librarian and Researcher Knowledge Space. 2022. https://www.ala.org/tools/research/larks/researchmethods.

Bhattacherjee, Anol. 2012. *Social Science Research: Principles, Methods, and Practices.* Second edition. Open Textbook Library. https://open.umn.edu/opentextbooks/BookDetail.aspx?bookId=79.

Brantlinger, Ellen, Robert Jimenez, Janette Klingner, Marleen Pugach, and Virginia Richardson. 2005. "Qualitative Studies in Special Education." *Exceptional Children* 71, no. 2: 195–207. https://doi.org/10.1177/001440290507100205.

Chu, Heting, and Qing Ke. 2017. "Research Methods: What's in the Name?" *Library & Information Science Research* 39, no. 4: 284–94. https://doi.org/10.1016/j.lisr.2017.11.001.

Crumley, Ellen, and Denise Koufogiannakis. 2002. "Developing Evidence-Based Librarianship: Practical Steps for Implementation." *Health Information & Libraries Journal* 19, no. 2: 61.

Eldredge, Jonathan D. 2004. "Inventory of Research Methods for Librarianship and Informatics." *J Med Libr Assoc* 92, no. 1: 83–90.

Given, Lisa M., ed. 2008. "Survey Research." In *The SAGE Encyclopedia of Qualitative Research Methods*. Thousand Oaks, CA: SAGE. https://doi.org/10.4135/9781412963909.n441.

Mills, Albert, Gabrielle Durepos, and Elden Wiebe, eds. 2010. "Quick Start to Case Study Research." In *Encyclopedia of Case Study Research*. Thousand Oaks, CA: SAGE. https://doi.org/10.4135/9781412957397.n283.

"Mixed Methods Research." 2022. Harvard Catalyst. https://catalyst.harvard.edu/community-engagement/mmr/.

Office for Human Research Protections. 2017. "2018 Requirements (2018 Common Rule)." Text. HHS.Gov. March 7. https://www.hhs.gov/ohrp/regulations-and-policy/regulations/45-cfr-46/revised-common-rule-regulatory-text/index.html.

"Research." 2003. In *McGraw-Hill Dictionary of Scientific and Technical Terms*, 6th ed. New York: McGraw-Hill Education. https://www-accessscience-com.proxy.li.suu.edu:2443/search?q=research&newSearch=Y.

"Research." 2022. In *OED Online*. Oxford University Press. http://www.oed.com/view/Entry/163432.

Salkind, Neil J., ed. 2010. "Quantitative Research." In *Encyclopedia of Research Design*. Thousand Oaks, CA: SAGE.

"Scientific Method." 2003. In *McGraw-Hill Dictionary of Scientific and Technical Terms*, 6th ed. New York: McGraw-Hill Education.

Smith, M. K. 2017. "What Is Action Research and How Do We Do It?—Infed.Org:" *The Encyclopedia of Pedagogy and Informal Education* (blog). 2017. https://infed.org/mobi/action-research/.

Stubeck, Carole J. 2015. "Enabling Inquiry Learning in Fixed-Schedule Libraries." *Knowledge Quest* 43, no. 3: 28–34.

Togia, Aspasia, and Afrodite Malliari. 2017. *Research Methods in Library and Information Science. Qualitative versus Quantitative Research*. London: IntechOpen. https://doi.org/10.5772/intechopen.68749.

5 Gathering Data and Descriptive Statistics

> **Essential Questions**
>
> Use these questions to guide your reading:
> - What is data and where can it be found?
> - How can original data be collected?
> - How do you protect, store, and share data?
> - What are descriptive statistics?

Introduction

Librarians tend to be efficient in collecting data. We collect data on nearly everything we do and, for things that we cannot collect data on, our vendors do it for us. We have data on gate counts, checkouts, reference questions, interlibrary loan requests received and sent, and so on. What do we do with all that data? We fill out forms and reports that ask how many things we have and how many times we did something. Do we even know why we collect it all? Are we making good use of our data? Can this data be used in research to help us learn about how well we are doing the things we do or what improvements could be made?

In the previous chapter, we looked at the research process and methodologies used to gather data for research. In this chapter, we will look at where and who collects data that we can use in our research. Then we will examine how we can collect and manage data generated by our research. Lastly, we will dive into descriptive statistics and use the data we collected to create a picture of our libraries and how they compare to others.

Your Library Data

Information is defined as "data which has been recorded, classified, organized, related, or interpreted within a framework so that meaning emerges" ("Information" 2003). This definition not only tells us what information is, but it also tells us what data is and is not. Data is not information. Data are the raw values that we make information from. It is unclassified, unorganized, and uninterpreted. We gather, organize, analyze, and interpret it to make sense of the story it tells. Data comes in two varieties as mentioned in the previous chapter: qualitative and quantitative. In her book on library data, Sandra Andrews defines qualitative and quantitative data. "Qualitative data is data that describes but does not measure … Quantitative data is numerical and measures a specific element" (2012, 3).

Library Management Systems

We have many sources for quantitative data. Our library management systems (LMS) are a great source of basic data about our libraries. They can tell us how many items are in our collection, what forms they take, how many were checked out, and how many library cardholders we have, and in what categories, such as student, teacher, or other classifications. Our LMSs have built-in report writers that allow us to create reports on the specific data we want.

Library Engagement Platform

Your library may have a Customer Relationship Management System, the business terminology for a library engagement platform (LEP). Regardless, an LEP is a software platform that serves to "make connections between the customer and our collections or between the customer and our library services" (King 2022, 7). They include an email system to reach out to patrons, but more importantly, they also include patron analytics that allows one to target a specific segment of customers with special messages about services and programs. The LEP tracks whom you sent what messages to and if they read it. It can manage and track your attendance at events and link that to how many emails were sent and to whom. Some like Gale Engage provide information on both physical and digital collection usage. Many will provide a dashboard to display current statistics. LEPs can be purchased from LMS vendors like OCLC (https://oclc.org/en/wise.html), SirsiDynix (https://www.sirsidynix.com/community-engagement-platform), and Innovative Interfaces (https://www.iii.com/products/vega), or from companies like BiblioCommons (https://www.bibliocommons.com), Patron Point (https://www.patronpoint.com), and Springshare (https://www.springshare.com/libcrm), to name a few. The platforms from the non-LMS vendors work with multiple systems. For more information on companies and their LEPs, consult the article by Marshall Breeding (2022) or contact the companies directly.

Most LEPs integrate with interlibrary loan (ILL) systems. ILL systems collect a lot of data about materials loaned or borrowed from other libraries. Cataloging systems can tell us how many items we cataloged. We may have a commercial system like LibAnswers (https://www.springshare.com/libanswers) to keep track of how many reference questions we answered in person, through chat, and what categories the questions fell into. Alternatively, we may use an Excel spreadsheet or a Google Form, or we may simply have a piece of paper with hash marks on it. We keep track of the number of instruction sessions we conduct, for whom we offer them, and how many people attended.

Knowing how many people use our libraries is valuable information. We may have an old-fashioned turnstile with a counter that needs to be read every morning by a staff member, or a high-tech security gate that sends information about how many people went in and out of the building to a website or database as well as recording the number of times the alarm went off when items that were not desensitized passed through the gate. We may take manual head counts to give us a better picture of how many people were in the library at a given time on a given day. We may be fortunate enough to have a system that reports and records our "traffic" data automatically.

Vendor-Provided Data

Most of our database vendors provide usage statistics in a standardized format known as COUNTER. These systems give us information on how many searches were run, the number of items found, and the number of full-text articles downloaded. Because the information adheres to a standard, we can directly compare our usage to another library's usage. Some database vendors have not yet embraced the COUNTER standard, but they still collect usage data that we can download. We may have a discovery layer searching all of our databases at once. It will provide us with usage information that may or may not be in the COUNTER format, but it will give us valuable information on how much our discovery layer is used and what databases get the most hits.

Our websites may use Google Analytics (https://analytics.google.com) or SiteImprove (https://www.siteimprove.com) among others to tell us how many hits each page in our website had, how long people stayed on our website, and from which page they exited our site. Programs like this can also tell us how many clicks it took people to get to a specific page. This is invaluable information for redesigning your website and bringing the most needed information up to the top to make it easier to find. For example, if the average number of clicks it takes to get the "chat with a librarian" page is four or more, you should consider moving it up or making it more visible. Maybe it has an icon on the home page, but people are not using it, because they do not understand what the symbol means.

Getting the information out of these various systems may take training or practice. Better yet, you may have an expert on staff who knows how to and would be happy to help you. To get information from a database vendor, you need to log into your account, navigate to the reports page, select the COUNTER report you want and the dates you want it for, then you will be able to download the report either directly to a spreadsheet or as a csv file that can be read by your spreadsheet program. It is not a difficult process, but if you have many vendors and many reports you want to download, it can take some time.

COUNTER reports include platform, database, book, journal, and multimedia. A platform report will show you how much activity you had on a particular vendor's platform. If you have multiple databases from that vendor, all the information is combined. If you have only one database, then the information in a platform report will represent the use of that database. Table 5.1 shows a platform report.

You can transpose the numbers and add a "totals" column, or you can use a pivot table in a spreadsheet program like Google Sheets or LibreOffice Calc (see Figure 5.1) to put all the information on one line and then add additional rows for each platform or vendor you have.

The database report provides similar information to the platform report. If you have multiple databases from one vendor, you will have multiple lines for each database from that vendor. Some vendors automatically search multiple databases at once without the user having selected them. In this case, you will get an additional line that shows those automatic searches.

In Table 5.2, some of the columns from the database report have been removed to simplify the information. Table 5.3 shows the data after applying a pivot table to show what may be a more useful format for the information.

The reports for books, journals, and media (TR_B1, TR_J1, and IR_M1) provide information about total item investigations and unique item requests. What is included in these reports may vary by publisher. However, if you use the appropriate Master Report, you can pick the data elements you want to be included such as total item investigations, unique items requests, and total item

Table 5.1 A COUNTER Platform, PR_P1, Report

Platform	Metric Type	Reporting Period Total	Jul	Aug	Sep	Oct	Nov	Dec	Jan	Feb	Mar	Apr	May	Jun
EX_p1	Unique_Title_Requests	26	0	0	3	0	0	3	2	5	5	8	0	0
EX_p1	Unique_Item_Requests	1,745	65	40	128	197	124	259	93	218	168	314	57	82
EX_p1	Total_Item_Requests	2,133	83	52	167	235	143	310	106	269	206	375	79	108
EX_p1	Searches_Platform	636	40	13	41	120	39	134	46	112	26	61	0	4

Source: Authors.

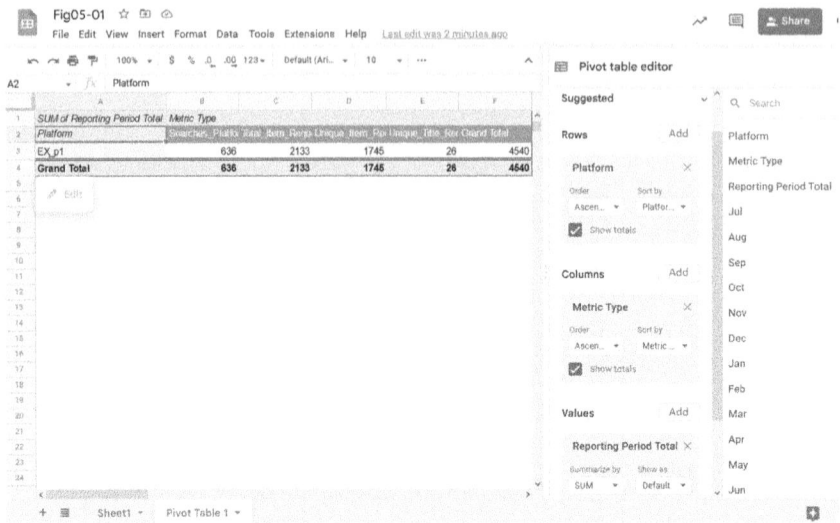

Figure 5.1 *Pivot table in Google Sheets.*
Source: Authors.

requests. A pivot table is, again, a good way to consolidate the information onto one line.

Project COUNTER (https://www.projectcounter.org/) is the official website of the COUNTER program. They have a lot of information for librarians and vendors. They also provide a simplified guide specifically for librarians, which describes each report, defines the terminology, and provides sample interpretations of reports to further clarify the meanings (Mellins-Cohen 2021).

Other Sources of Library Data

There is a tremendous amount of data available about communities, school districts, and libraries. Your research may be based on this information or use this information to supplement and give context to the original data that you collect. The first type of data you may need is information about your community: population, income, employment. Here, the census has you covered. The US Census Bureau (US Census Bureau n.d.) collects all kinds of data from what you would find in County Business Patterns and the Economic Census to the decennial census and its updates in the American Community Survey. The interface to the information has changed regularly in the past. Now, the population information can be found on the Census' data site ("Census Bureau Data" n.d.) where you can enter search

Table 5.2 A COUNTER Database, DR_D1, Report

Database	Metric_Type	Reporting Period Total	Jul	Aug	Sep	Oct	Nov	Dec	Jan	Feb	Mar	Apr	May	Jun
EX_db1	Searches_Automated	819	29	13	67	148	84	61	63	82	96	82	41	53
EX_db1	Total_Item_Investigations	33	0	1	0	5	7	1	0	1	7	3	1	7
EX_db1	Total_Item_Requests	31	0	1	0	3	7	1	0	1	7	3	1	7
EX_db2	Total_Item_Investigations	130	0	1	0	26	12	6	15	21	15	9	20	5
EX_db2	Total_Item_Requests	121	0	1	0	21	12	6	15	21	15	9	16	5
EX_db2	Searches_Regular	855	32	13	68	156	85	61	72	87	103	84	41	53
EX_db3	Searches_Automated	1,211	38	35	124	187	145	71	157	123	137	92	44	58
EX_db3	Searches_Regular	1	0	0	0	0	0	0	0	0	0	0	1	0
EX_db3	Total_Item_Investigations	612	5	11	154	16	15	7	148	56	118	28	31	23
EX_db3	Total_Item_Requests	595	5	9	153	16	15	7	146	50	116	25	30	23

Source: Authors.

terms to find specific information about your community, or you can drill down through a map and receive a profile with general population information about the selected entity, state, county, or city. Figure 5.2 shows the income and poverty information for Chicago ("Chicago City, Illinois—Census Bureau Profile" n.d.).

Data is available in tables, which can be downloaded in multiple formats. Table 5.4 shows educational attainment for Sioux Falls, South Dakota ("DP02: Selected Social Characteristics in Sioux Falls, South Dakota" n.d.).

The US government also collects specific data on libraries. The National Center for Educational Statistics (NCES) collects all kinds of data related to education. For

Table 5.3 *A Pivot Table of the Database Data*

SUM of Reporting Period Total	Metric Type				
Database	Searches Automated	Searches Regular	Total Item Investigations	Total Item Requests	Grand Total
EX_db1	819		33	31	883
EX_db2		855	130	121	1,106
EX_db3	1,211	1	612	595	2,419
Grand Total	2,030	856	775	747	4,408

Source: Authors.

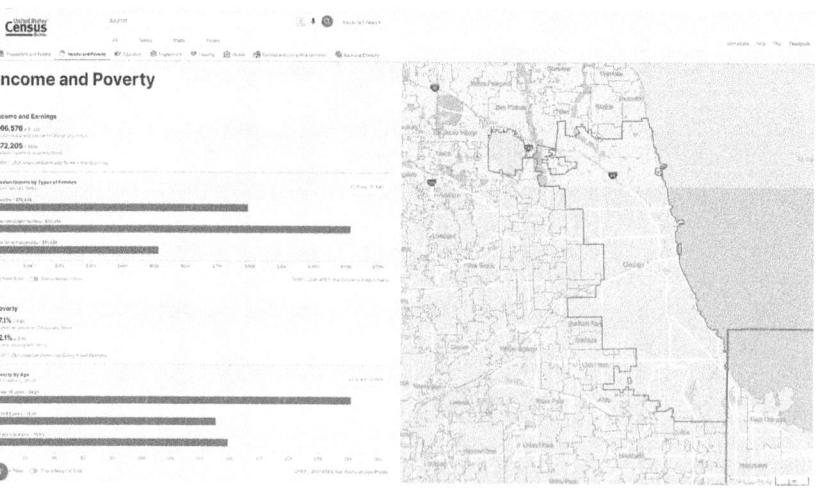

Figure 5.2 *Income and poverty information for Chicago, Illinois. United States Census Bureau. Source: United States Census Bureau. www.census.gov.*

Table 5.4 *Educational Attainment for Sioux Falls, South Dakota*

Label	Sioux Falls city, South Dakota			
	Estimate	Margin of Error	Percent	Percent Margin of Error
Educational Attainment				
Population 25 years and over	123,757	±672	123,757	(X)
Less than 9th grade	3,515	±492	2.80%	±0.4
9th to 12th grade, no diploma	4,760	±644	3.80%	±0.5
High school graduate (includes equivalency)	30,438	±1,452	24.60%	±1.1
Some college, no degree	25,424	±1,343	20.50%	±1.1
Associate's degree	15,078	±949	12.20%	±0.8
Bachelor's degree	30,106	±1,056	24.30%	±0.9
Graduate or professional degree	14,436	±1,219	11.70%	±1.0
High school graduate or higher	115,482	±1,131	93.30%	±0.7
Bachelor's degree or higher	44,542	±1,580	36.00%	±1.3

Source: Authors.

academic libraries, the Integrated Postsecondary Education Data System (IPEDS) ("Integrated Postsecondary Education Data System" n.d.) is of primary importance. It collects information about colleges and universities, and their libraries. Universities generally have a list of peer institutions, schools that are roughly equivalent, that they use for comparative purposes. IPEDS lets you select multiple institutions and the data elements you want. For example, you can select all the information about academic libraries and add in the full-time equivalent (FTE) enrollment.

Table 5.5 shows data for a college and four of its peer institutions for the most recent year. The colleges have been anonymized. The data give you a way to compare one institution to another. By including the FTE data, you can use a ratio to level the comparative playing field. We will talk a little more about ratios in the Descriptive Statistics section of this chapter below.

The Institute of Museum and Library Services (ILMS) conducts the Public Libraries Survey. Data is collected from public libraries in every state, territory,

Table 5.5 IPEDS Data for Five Universities

Selected IPEDS Data	Librarians FTE	Other Professional FTE Staff	Number of Physical Books	Number of Digital/Electronic Books	Total Physical Library Circulations	Total Materials/ Services Expenditures	FTE Fall Enrollment
Your Institution	10.0	7.3	210,475	279,602	35,287	$385,376	10,580
Peer Institution 1	12.0	0.0	199,513	433,623	8,570	$771,653	7,378
Peer Institution 2	8.0	8.0	218,808	666,273	10,139	$652,810	4,520
Peer Institution 3	4.8	13.3	410,329	268,078	4,228	$458,156	3,705
Peer Institution 4	8.0	1.0	339,560	271,957	22,879	$951,772	3,757

Source: Authors.

and the District of Columbia and includes visits, circulations, size of collections, staffing, expenditures, and other data points ("Public Libraries Survey" n.d.). Data can be downloaded as a CSV file to be used with a spreadsheet or as either SAS or SPSS to be used with those statistical analysis programs.

You cannot pick and choose locations or data elements to download. You have to download the entire dataset. As a result, the files are large. Abbreviations are used in the headers. The meaning of some may be obvious, but it is best to download the user guide as well (Pelczar et al. 2022). It not only explains the abbreviations, but it also provides extensive additional information about the survey, data collection methods, the survey itself, and response rates. The data comes in three files. The smallest is aggregated data by state. The other two files are alphabetized by city within the state. The smaller of the two contains data on how many hours the library is open, how many weeks it is open, and the square footage of the library. The largest file has the bulk of the statistics dealing with collections, staffing, and budgets. It also includes the population of the library service area and the number of bookmobiles. The information contained in these files is invaluable for comparative purposes. Table 5.6 shows a small sample of the public library statistics taken from the IMLS data. It includes reference transactions, the number of registered borrowers, and total circulations.

The NCES also has statistics about school libraries as part of the National Teacher and Principal Survey (NTPS) ("National Teacher and Principal Survey" n.d.). On the Table List page, you will find a handful of tables that mention school libraries. The

Table 5.6 *IMLS Data Sample for Public Libraries*

REFERENCE	F_REFER	REFERRPT	REGBOR	F_REGBOR	TOTCIR
12412	R_20	CT	43490	R_20	116239
45021	R_20	CT	45271	R_20	681102
3120	R_20	ES	6005	R_20	139664
16849	R_20	CT	34461	R_20	597006
109952	R_20	CT	318880	R_20	744300
544	R_20	ES	5537	R_20	19831
49880	R_20	CT	46902	R_20	303050
11602	R_20	CT	7016	R_20	123702
29221	R_20	CT	173903	R_20	847270
290542	R_20	CT	373621	R_20	2238705

Source: Authors.

information is aggregated at the national and state levels. Take note of the dates. It takes a while to collect and organize the information. The most recent table is five years old. The Common Core of Data (CCD), also at the NCES site, has more current data aggregated at both the state and national levels ("Common Core of Data" n.d.). It is harder to use, requiring some trial and error, and exploration to find what you are looking for.

The NCES also provides a way to find school districts and specific schools within a district. The district and school locator are also part of the CCD website. They provide very general information about the district or school: number of students, number of teachers, and student/teacher ratio. The school level also breaks enrollment down by grade, race/ethnicity, and gender. More importantly, it provides the web address for the district and the school. This will allow you to find more information. There is even a search resource that lets you drill down on a map to select either a district or a school ("CCD School Map" n.d.).

School and district data may be gathered in one place at the state level, or it may not. How states collect and share data varies widely. Districts collect data on test scores, enrollment, demographics, library collection size, and age (Andrews 2012, 3). You will have to do some online research to see what you can find. You can also ask colleagues and administrators for local school data and district data.

Your Research Data

When thinking about your research project, perhaps the data you need has not already been collected and made available by outside sources. Perhaps you want to use some data from government agencies to augment the data you need to collect from students or patrons of your library. Perhaps the only source of data that will work for your research project is data that you specifically collect to inform your project.

When you start planning your research, you need to identify your data needs and develop a data management plan (DMP). You need to decide what type of information you need to collect to support your research and from whom you will collect the data. Will you use Google Forms (https://www.google.com/forms/about/), Survey Monkey (https://www.surveymonkey.com/), or Qualtrics (https://www.qualtrics.com/) to send out and collect survey data? Will you use your Learning Management System, like Canvas (https://www.instructure.com/canvas),

Blackboard (https://www.blackboard.com/group/141), or Moodle (https://moodle.org/) to collect test or survey data? If you are going to use paper forms, where will they be handed out and collected? Who will input the information into a spreadsheet? If some or all of the data is qualitative, how are you going to analyze it? Will you use software? Will multiple people be involved in reading and interpreting text-based answers, and if so, how will you train them to analyze the information in the same manner?

You need to consider whether the data can be collected anonymously, and if not, how you will ensure the privacy of your participants. Remember that "it is not appropriate or legal to share identifiable, individual student data" (Andrews 2012, 22). You need to plan to remove identifiable data to ensure student and patron privacy. This process is called de-identifying your data. Your LEP may be able to provide highly specific data like the number of patrons in the northwest service area making between $50,000 and $70,000 per year, aged between forty and forty-five years old who are female, and check out more than two science fiction books per week, but that might be only one or two people. They would be easily identifiable, and such a narrow piece of information with so few people will not provide enough information to help you with any research project.

Creating a Data Management Plan

You need to plan for how your data will be stored, for how long, and who will have access to it. If you collect your data on paper with identifying data, you need to keep it in a locking file cabinet so that you, as the primary investigator, can ensure sole access. If you convert the paper to digital, you can destroy the paper, but there are still important considerations for storing digital information.

There are legal requirements for storing some types of information. Be sure to consult with your IRB to see what you have to do. Sites like this one from the University of Florida (https://irb.ufl.edu/index/data/investigator-requirements-for-retaining-research-data.html) will tell you how long you need to store data based on what types of data you are collecting and from whom you may have received a grant for your research. For example, typically research data needs to be saved for three years after the completion of the research, but identifiable medical data needs to be stored for six years (Institutional Review Board, University of Florida 2023). Your university, school, or library may have additional requirements, and even publishers may require you to store data for a certain period of time. Be sure to find out all the requirements before you start collecting your data.

Storing data digitally brings up other issues. You may need to limit access to the data files through encryption to authorized people only ("Research Data Storage and Retention" 2022). You may want to keep it on a flash drive that is password-protected with the file itself encrypted. You may not even want to put digital information onto a computer connected to the web—and definitely not in the cloud until any possible identifying information is removed. Even then, it is a good idea to keep the information under lock and key until you are ready to share it with the world.

There are guides available to help you plan your data management strategy. The Inter-University Consortium for Political and Social Research (ICPSR) has a framework that spells out the elements of a DMP that includes items like ethics and privacy, format, security, and legal requirements ("Framework for Creating a Data Management Plan" 2023). The Utrecht Data School in the Netherlands has a Data Ethics Decision Aid poster and guide to help you answer essential questions about working with your data ("Data Ethics Decision Aid (DEDA)" 2023).

The National Institutes of Health (NIH) has a data management and sharing policy that requires all research that they funded or even partially funded to share their data ("Data Management and Sharing Policy" n.d.). Their site also includes information on data management, budgeting for sharing data, and a list of possible repositories where you can share your data. They also give guidance on what data needs to be shared and what does not or should not be shared (Federer 2023). While most of us will not be doing research that the NIH funds, their website offers valuable information on DMPs that will help us create a plan and successfully share our data.

You can use DMPTool (https://dmptool.org/) which is designed to help you create a DMP. You need to create an account to use the tool. Once you have signed up, you can create a DMP by using their tabbed series of forms that asks questions like "What data will you collect or create?" and "How will the data be collected or created?" Each question comes with guidance on what you need to consider to formulate an answer (California Digital Library 2023).

The Research and Assessment Cycle Toolkit (https://www.arl.org/research-and-assessment-cycle-toolkit/) from the Association of Research Libraries is designed for librarians and library staff to use when assessing library programs, services, and resources. It includes short videos on all aspects of the research and assessment cycle like collecting data through interviews, focus groups, and surveys; analyzing data; and reflecting on and communicating results (Association of Research Libraries n.d.). It is a unique and helpful resource.

Sharing Your Data

Sharing your data is an important aspect of the research process. "Researchers spend considerable time, money, and effort collecting and interrogating data. Making your data discoverable, accessible, interoperable, and reusable (FAIR) maximises [sic] the impact of that investment" ("FAIR Data" 2022). The FAIR data principles were first published by a group of scholars in 2016. "Good data management is not a goal in itself, but rather is the key conduit leading to knowledge discovery and innovation, and to subsequent data and knowledge integration and reuse by the community after the data publication process" (Wilkinson et al. 2016, 1). Sharing our data improves the reproducibility and reliability of research, enables new research and partnerships, and supports new discoveries through new uses and meta-analysis of your data. It is an essential piece of open science that will improve your visibility as a researcher, as well.

Your DMP should include where you are going to store your data and the metadata tags you are going to use to describe your data to make it easily findable by others. Some journals may require that you share your data in their data repository. Additionally, you can store your data in another data repository that allows your data to be found and used by other researchers. The Center for Open Science's (COS) mission is to "increase openness, integrity, and reproducibility of research" (Nosek et al. 2017). COS administers the Open Science Foundation (OSF) (https://osf.io/) where you can create an account, store, and share your research with others. Their repository will even help you create metadata for your data file to make it more findable and usable by others. You can use OSF as a collaborative space to work with colleagues and use their preprint service to publish your report ("OSF" 2023). OSF is a free service that provides a large amount of storage space. ICPSR has a data repository. Your university may have a data repository or belong to a consortium that has a repository. Be sure to look for a repository that fits your needs.

Open science is going even further. There is now a drive for open notebook science. This practice encourages researchers to put all of their research including each step in the research process online in a shared repository. This type of sharing is named for the lab notebook that researchers use to record the day-to-day progress of their research ("Open-Notebook Science" 2022). Openlabnotebooks.org promotes this idea. They believe that "making our research, data, and protocols available on a day-to-day basis will generate scientific ideas and discussions, avoid redundancy, foster collaborations, and accelerate progress" ("Welcome to Open Lab Notebooks." 2023).

Some journals are now allowing you to register your research with them before you begin to do it. Your research proposal would undergo a peer-review process, and if accepted, your report is guaranteed, with some caveats, to be published (Riegelman 2021). Registered reports are an important development for researchers. First, you get feedback on your research plan and suggestions for improvements. Second, this method helps avoid some issues with research and publication, like publication bias. This is where either a journal will only publish a paper if it has positive, statistically significant results, or a researcher, fearing that no one will publish their negative results, does not bother to send their research to a journal for consideration. A negative finding can be very useful and important to others and needs to be published. A number of publishers, journals, and the COS accept registered reports (Center for Open Science n.d.; Springer Nature 2023).

Your DMP will help you organize your research and data collection. It may also help other researchers and the profession when you consider participating in open science.

Descriptive Statistics

The data sources mentioned in Sharing Your Data contain descriptive statistics. A descriptive statistic is a quantitative summary of an item or action. It could be how many books you have in your library, how many books you bought, and how many books you circulated last year. Descriptive statistics are how we analyze those data summaries.

Descriptive statistics include measures of central tendency, which is the statistician's way of saying averages, the standard deviation, which is the range or spread in the data, or more formally, the dispersion of the data, and normality of the distribution that relates to the appearance of the data. The normal distribution of data follows a bell curve. You can use your favorite spreadsheet to do these types of calculations. However, we are going to use an open-source program called jamovi (https://www.jamovi.org/). We will talk more about jamovi in Chapter 7 when we discuss inferential statistics.

You can use your summary data statistics to compare your library to another. This can be a useful way to see what other organizations are doing differently. You can compare your library to a group of peers to see where your strengths and weaknesses lie. However, these may not be "apples-to-apple" comparisons, as differences in budgets or populations served will skew the results.

You can make the comparisons more appropriate with a little division. Ratios are a great way to level out differences. You can divide the material expenditures of each library by the number of people served to generate spending per patron. If your school has a material budget of $100,000 while a peer institution has a budget of $200,000, dividing the material budget by the FTE enrollment takes into account the difference between enrollment and yields a number that shows material expenditures per pupil. If that peer institution has twice as many FTEs as your school, then expenditures per student are the same. An expenditure of $100,000/1,000 students is the same as $200,000/2,000 students, or $100 expended per student. If they have the same number of students as your school, then their budget allows them to spend twice as much money per student as you do. $200,000/1,000 students equals $200 expended per student. You can do the same calculations with circulation to see how many items your library circulates per person versus your peers. For example, if your school has 500 students, and circulates 2,000 books, then you are circulating an average of 4 books per student. If a peer school has 750 students and circulates 6,000 books, then they are circulating an average of 8 books per student. You may want to dig through more data to see if you can figure out why their circulation rate is higher. Could it be the respective ages of the collections, the sizes of the collections, or something else entirely?

Descriptive statistics include three measures of central tendency: the mean, the median, and the mode. The mean is the average number of visitors to your library in a month or a week, or it is the average number of reference transactions you have each hour. Below, in Figure 5.3, is an example of the mean and median for reference transactions. It shows that reference is staffed seven hours a day. The first couple and last couple of hours are not as busy as the mid-day hours. jamovi includes an editor on the spreadsheet side, where you can type in information.

To download the jamovi program, go to https://www.jamovi.org/download.html. Chromebooks need additional setup to run the program. The jamovi user guide (https://www.jamovi.org/user-manual.html#linux-and-chromebooks) has basic instructions, but unless you have already set up a Linux environment within your Chromebook, you will need to do that (https://flatpak.org/setup/Chrome%20OS) before you can install the program (https://flathub.org/apps/details/org.jamovi.jamovi) ("User Guide" n.d.; "Chrome OS Quick Setup" n.d.; "Jamovi" n.d.).

We entered the service hours in the first column and the number of questions received in the second column. The Exploration tab is where descriptive statistics are found. After making a few choices, we receive the output (Figure 5.3).

The mean or average number of reference questions received in an hour is 8.57. The median is 6. The median is the number in the middle of the range. If we organized the seven results for the number of questions from lowest to highest, then looked at the fourth number in the sequence that is the number in the

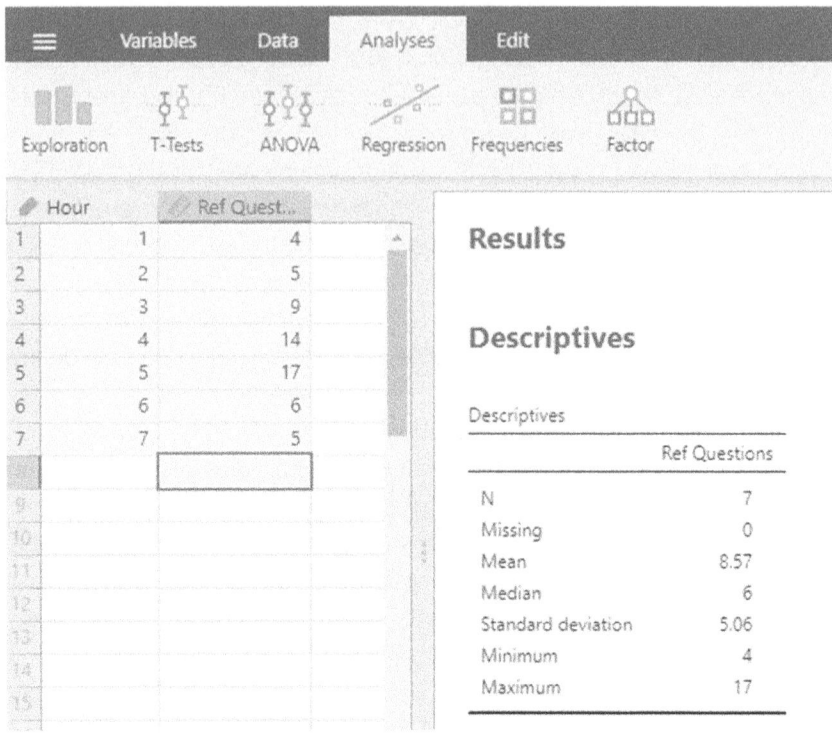

Figure 5.3 *Mean and median for reference.*
Source: jamovi.

middle, we have 6. The median is useful when you have one or two numbers that are very high or very low and skew the average. An example would be when you calculate the average librarian's salary—as your director receives a very high salary, it will inflate the average salary and give the wrong impression. In this case, it might be better to look at the median salary.

Figure 5.3 also shows the minimum and maximum number of questions that give you the range of your data from 4 to 17. The standard deviation is also calculated. The standard deviation shows the amount of variance in the data relative to the mean or average. Standard deviation may be abbreviated as *SD* or as the Greek letter sigma, σ. In this case, it is about 5. This means that most of the time when you are working at the reference desk you can expect to have about nine reference questions, plus or minus five, or four to thirteen. Another way to think about it is given a normal distribution, 68 percent of the time, you will get four to thirteen questions at the reference desk. A small standard deviation means there is little variability in the numbers, while a large standard deviation means that there is greater variability and less consistency in the numbers.

The mode is the final measure of central tendency. It is the item that appears most in your data set. In Figure 5.3, the number of questions that shows up the most is 5. That is the mode of our reference questions. However, five only appears twice in our data and may not be very useful here. However, the mode will show you the most chosen answer to a survey question. If you ask your patrons how they would rate the helpfulness of the librarian and the most popular answer is "extremely helpful," that can be useful information.

The normal distribution refers to a standard bell curve and how much of your data lies under certain parts of it. Many statistical tests are based on the idea that the data follows a normal distribution. In the normal distribution, 68 percent of the data falls within plus or minus one standard deviation of the mean, 95 percent of the data lies within two standard deviations, and 99.7 percent falls within three standard deviations. See Figure 5.4.

There are multiple graphs available from the Exploration tab in jamovi. The histogram will help you visualize your data and make a determination of its normality. It is a frequency distribution which means it shows how often values occur. It uses bars to represent a range of values. The example in Figure 5.5 is taken from one of the sample datasets included with jamovi. It shows a normal distribution.

A Q-Q plot, which stands for quantile-quantile, is another visual method to see how normal your data is. The more your data follows a line, the more normal it is. As Clay Ford points out, it is not a proof, and its interpretation is "somewhat

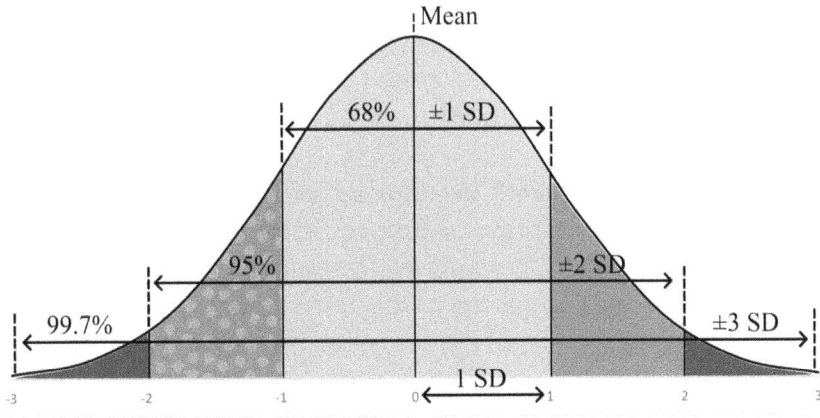

Figure 5.4 *The standard distribution.*
Source: jamovi.

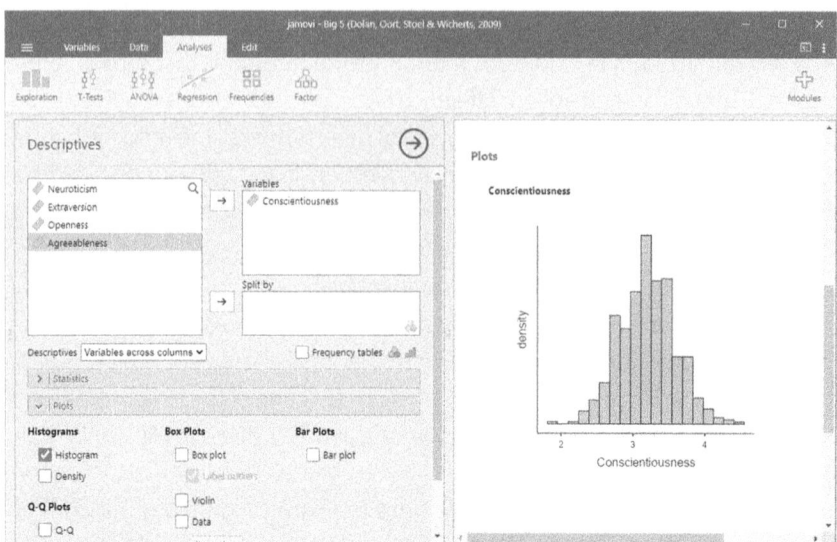

Figure 5.5 *Histogram of the Big 5 dataset from jamovi.*
Source: jamovi.

subjective" (2015). This is the case with histograms as well. You can see in Figure 5.6 that the data is very linear, indicating that it is normal.

A box plot, or box and whisker plot, shows your data divided into quartiles. The box in the middle is divided into the second and third quartiles by a line representing the median value. The lower half of the box shows the range of values that represent 25–50 percent of the data, while the top half of the box represents 50–75 percent of the data. The whiskers show the first quartile and the fourth quartile representing the lowest and highest 25 percent of the data. Box plots also show you outliers, values that are much higher or lower than the other values. The box plot in Figure 5.7 shows that data is clustered in the middle quartiles with somewhat long whiskers and four outliers, two above and two below the whiskers.

Outliers need to be examined. They could be caused by data collection errors. If that is the case, you need to see if you can correct the data or, if not, exclude it from the set of information. They could represent anomalies or natural variations in the data or indicate that the data is skewed and needs to be kept as part of the dataset. Skewed data means that the normal distribution is pushed to one side or the other. If the data is skewed, you may need to consider statistical tests that can handle that kind of data. You could have given a quiz, and it was easy. The results are skewed from normal because most students scored better than 85 percent.

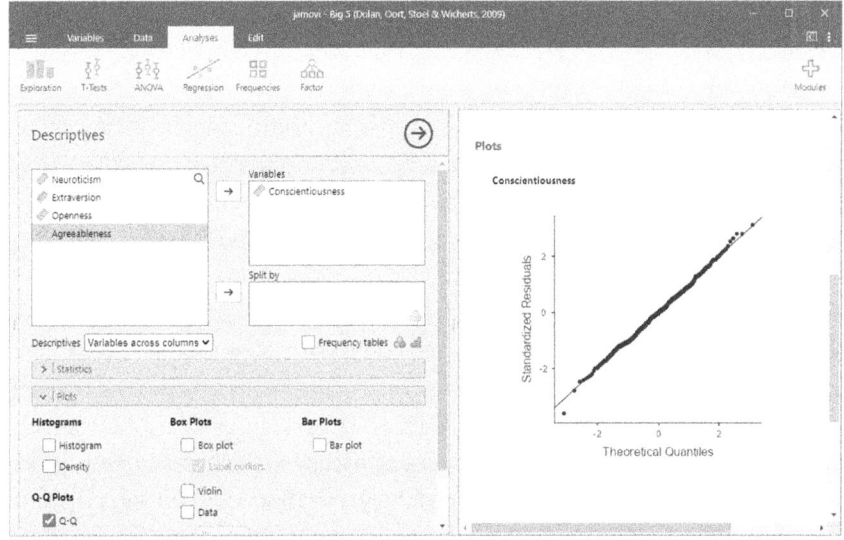

Figure 5.6 *Q-Q plot of the Big 5 dataset from jamovi.*
Source: jamovi.

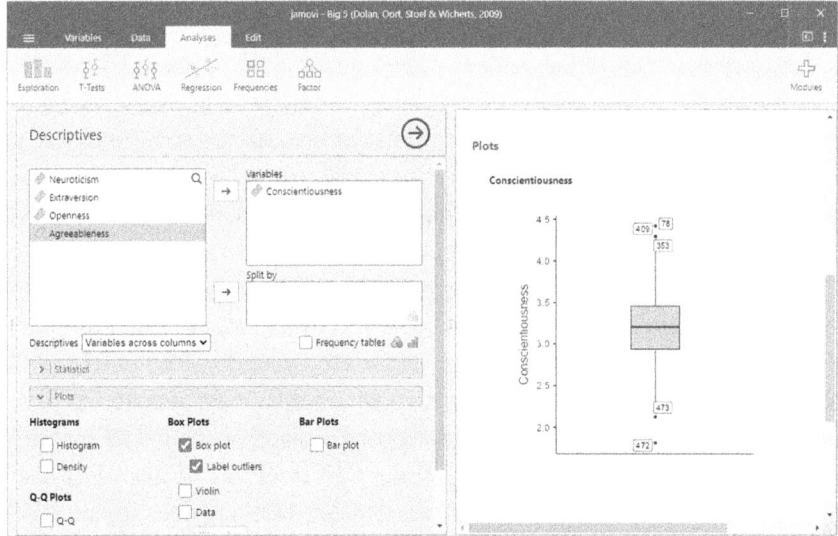

Figure 5.7 *Box plot of the Big 5 dataset from jamovi.*
Source: jamovi.

Not all data analysis needs to be complicated to prove useful to your institution and to the profession. Descriptive statistics can paint a picture of your library and provide valuable feedback on how your library is performing and what could be improved in the future. Research articles may contain nothing but descriptive statistics and provide useful, actionable information to others. An older study showed that 83 percent of library research with statistical analysis used descriptive statistics (Hildreth and Aytac 2007). One of the authors updated the study and found that about 74 percent of the research articles used descriptive statistics (Aytac and Slutsky 2014). A study of research articles published in two school library journals showed that more than half of the research used descriptive statistics (Morris and Cahill 2017). While this shows a trend toward inferential statistics that will be covered in Chapter 7, it still indicates that useful research does not have to involve complex statistical analysis. An example of that is an article written by Scales, Turner-Rahman, and Hao, which examined reference statistics gathered from different service points and via different methods (in person, chat) to draw conclusions about where, when, and how to staff the reference service desks (2015).

Summary and Reflection

In this chapter, we looked at some common sources of data about your library and other libraries. We examined what the data looks like and talked about how it can be used. A tremendous amount of data can be collected about your library through descriptive statistics that show how much your collections, services, and programs were used. Supplemental data about your community can be gathered from the census, or your existing institution data. Does your library already have the data you need for your research project? If not, how will you collect it?

When thinking about your data, you need to develop a DMP that answers all the questions about gathering, storing, and sharing your data. You need a DMP to ensure your research process goes smoothly. Are you also required to have one because your research is being funded by a grant? You need to consider patron privacy and legal issues as part of your plan. Does your library have a data repository where you can store and share your data? Do you need to find one? Does the journal you sent your manuscript to require you to share your data to their repository? Consider these questions and make a plan before moving forward with your research to prevent issues down the line.

Lastly, we discussed descriptive statistics, what they are, and some ways to work with them. Descriptive statistics provide valuable information to help you and your colleagues make informed decisions about library services, budgets, and beyond. When you think about the research you want to do, will descriptive statistics be enough to answer your questions? Will you learn enough from averages, percentiles, ratios, and comparisons? If not, inferential statistics will be covered in this text as well.

Implementation

Using the sites mentioned above, build a DMP for your potential research. You can be more or less detailed based on whether you are beginning to work on a research project or are just thinking about doing one. Where will you find the data? What considerations need to be made for how you will collect and store the data? Find a list of repositories or a list of repository lists like this one (https://www.library.ucsb.edu/scholarly-communication/open-access-repositories) from the University of California, Santa Barbara, and identify one or two possible repositories for your research. Visit the repository and look for information on how to format and submit your data.

Find descriptive statistics for your library for your most recent year and four or five years prior. Compare the numbers. What factors may have contributed to the changes you see? More students? Smaller budget? Longer hours? Where can you find the additional information to prove your hypothesis? Look at a number for any one of your services. Think about all the changes you could make in your library that would increase the size of that number next year. How would you evaluate the one change you like best to see if it really did increase that number?

Vocabulary

Box plot
Customer relationship management system
Data
Data management plan
Data repository
De-identifying data
Descriptive statistics
FAIR
Histogram
IMLS

IPEDS
Library engagement platform
Mean
Measures of central tendency
Median
Mode
NCES
Normal distribution
Open science
Outliers
Q-Q plots
Quartiles
Ratios
Standard deviation

References

Andrews, Sandra D. 2012. *The Power of Data: An Introduction to Using Local, State, and National Data to Support School Library Programs*. Chicago: American Association of School Librarians. http://site.ebrary.com/id/10604645.

Association of Research Libraries. n.d. "Research and Assessment Cycle Toolkit." https://www.arl.org/research-and-assessment-cycle-toolkit/. Accessed November 3, 2022.

Aytac, Selenay, and Bruce Slutsky. 2014. "Published Librarian Research, 2008 through 2012: Analyses and Perspectives." *Collaborative Librarianship* 6, no. 4: 147–59.

Breeding, Marshall. 2022. "Assembling a Patron Engagement Ecosystem." *Library Technology Reports* 58, no. 2: 16–17.

California Digital Library. 2023. "DMPTool." https://dmptool.org/.

"CCD School Map." n.d. National Center for Education Statistics. https://nces.ed.gov/ccd/schoolmap/. Accessed January 4, 2023.

"Census Bureau Data." n.d. https://data.census.gov/. Accessed December 28, 2022.

Center for Open Science. n.d. "Registered Reports." Center for Open Science. https://www.cos.io/initiatives/registered-reports. Accessed January 16, 2023.

"Chicago City, Illinois—Census Bureau Profile." n.d. https://data.census.gov/profile?g=1600000US1714000. Accessed December 28, 2022.

"Common Core of Data." n.d. National Center for Education Statistics. National Center for Education Statistics. https://nces.ed.gov/ccd/. Accessed January 3, 2023.

"Data Ethics Decision Aid (DEDA)." 2023. Utrecht Data School. https://dataschool.nl/en/deda/.

"Data Management and Sharing Policy." n.d. Scientific Data Sharing. https://sharing.nih.gov/data-management-and-sharing-policy. Accessed January 20, 2023.

"DP02: Selected Social Characteristics in Sioux Falls, South Dakota." n.d. https://data.census.gov/table?g=1600000US4659020&tid=ACSDP5Y2021.DP02. Accessed December 28, 2022.

"FAIR Data." 2022. Australian Research Data Commons. May 12. https://ardc.edu.au/resource/fair-data/.

Federer, Lisa. 2023. "An Overview of the National Institutes of Health (NIH) Data Management and Sharing Policy." January 11. https://doi.org/10.5281/zenodo.7535199.

Ford, Clay. 2015. "Understanding Q-Q Plots." University of Virginia Library Research Data Services + Sciences. August 26. https://data.library.virginia.edu/understanding-q-q-plots/.

"Framework for Creating a Data Management Plan." 2023. ICPSR. https://www.icpsr.umich.edu/web/pages/datamanagement/dmp/framework.html.

Hildreth, Charles R., and Selenay Aytac. 2007. "Recent Library Practitioner Research: A Methodological Analysis and Critique." *Journal of Education for Library & Information Science* 48, no. 3: 236–58.

"Information." 2003. In *McGraw-Hill Dictionary of Scientific and Technical Terms*, 6th ed. New York: McGraw-Hill.

Institutional Review Board, University of Florida. 2023. "Investigator Requirements for Retaining Research Data." Institutional Review Board. https://irb.ufl.edu/index/data/investigator-requirements-for-retaining-research-data.html.

"Integrated Postsecondary Education Data System." n.d. National Center for Education Statistics. https://nces.ed.gov/ipeds/. Accessed December 28, 2022.

The jamovi project (n.d.). Jamovi (Version 2.3) [Computer Software]. https://www.jamovi.org.

King, David Lee. 2022. "Library Engagement Platforms." *Library Technology Reports* 58, no. 1: 1–29.

Mellins-Cohen, Tasha. 2021. "Release 5.0.2: The Friendly Guide for Librarians." COUNTER. https://medialibrary.projectcounter.org/file/The-Friendly-Guide-for-Librarians.

Morris, Rebecca J., and Maria Cahill. 2017. "A Study of How We Study: Methodologies of School Library Research 2007 through July 2015." *School Library Research* 20 (January): 1–29.

"National Teacher and Principal Survey." n.d. National Center for Education Statistics. National Center for Education Statistics. https://nces.ed.gov/surveys/ntps/. Accessed January 3, 2023.

Nosek, Brian A., Lisa Cuevas Shaw, Timothy M. Errington, Nicole Pfeiffer, David Thomas Mellor, Ronald E. Brooks Iii, Alexis Rice, and David M. Litherland. 2017. "Center for Open Science: Strategic Plan." OSF Preprints. https://doi.org/10.31219/osf.io/x2w9h.

"Open-Notebook Science." 2022. In *Wikipedia*. https://en.wikipedia.org/w/index.php?title=Open-notebook_science&oldid=1105746365.

"OSF." 2023. https://osf.io/.

Pelczar, Marisa, Jake Soffronoff, Evan Nielsen, Jiayi Li, and Sam Mabile. 2022. *Data File Documentation and User's Guide: Public Libraries in the United States Fiscal Year 2020*. Washington, DC: Institute of Museum and Library Services. https://www.imls.gov/sites/default/files/2022-07/2020_pls_data_file_documentation.pdf.

"Public Libraries Survey." n.d. Institute of Museum and Library Services. http://www.imls.gov/research-evaluation/data-collection/public-libraries-survey. Accessed December 26, 2022.

"Research Data Storage and Retention." 2022. *Elsevier Author Services – Articles* (blog). January 4, 2022. https://scientific-publishing.webshop.elsevier.com/publication-process/research-data-storage-retention/.

Riegelman, Amy. 2021. "Considering Registered Reports at C&RL." *College & Research Libraries* 82, no. 1: 2–6. https://doi.org/10.5860/crl.82.1.2.

Scales, B. Jane, Lipi Turner-Rahman, and Feng Hao. 2015. "A Holistic Look at Reference Statistics: Whither Librarians?" *Evidence Based Library and Information Practice* 10, no. 4: 173. https://doi.org/10.18438/B8X01H.

Springer Nature. 2023. "Registered Reports." Scientific Reports. https://www.nature.com/srep/journal-policies/registered-reports.

US Census Bureau. n.d. "Census.Gov." Census.Gov. https://www.census.gov/en.html. Accessed December 28, 2022.

"Welcome to Open Lab Notebooks." 2023. Openlabnotebooks.Org. https://openlabnotebooks.org/.

Wilkinson, Mark D., Michel Dumontier, IJsbrand Jan Aalbersberg, Gabrielle Appleton, Myles Axton, Arie Baak, Niklas Blomberg, et al. 2016. "The FAIR Guiding Principles for Scientific Data Management and Stewardship." *Scientific Data* 3, no. 1: 160018. https://doi.org/10.1038/sdata.2016.18.

6 Statistical Significance, Effect Size, and Power

> **Essential Questions**
>
> Use these questions to guide your reading:
> - What is statistics?
> - What key concepts are most important to doing research?
> - What is statistical significance?
> - How does sample size and effect size affect significance?

Introduction

In the previous chapter, we talked about gathering, protecting, sharing, and storing data as well as using descriptive statistics. The statistical concepts in Chapter 5 were as follows: measure of central tendency, dispersion, ratios, and percentages through quartiles. In this chapter, we will start to examine some important concepts that are central to statistical analysis, but we will hold off on inferential statistics until the next chapter.

One of the goals of this book is to take some of the hesitation out of conducting statistical analyses. A recent study by Park showed that master's-level students in sociology take on average 2.7 research method courses, while MLIS students take 0.6 of a course. Further, the study showed that 64 percent of the time in sociology research method courses was devoted to statistical analysis, while the MLIS courses spent only 19 percent of the time dealing with statistical analysis (2022, 224). This lack of exposure, along with all the mathematical equations and jargon that goes along with statistics, no doubt plays a role in any hesitation you may have encountered regarding this topic. In this chapter, we will examine the concept of statistical significance as a first step in understanding statistics.

Statistics

Our lives are full of numbers. We hear and see statistics from the news media. We deal with numbers whenever we shop. We look up the chances of getting side effects from a new prescription. We wonder what the impact of higher interest rates will be on our ability to buy a new house. It is important to know where our numbers come from and what they mean.

For our libraries, profession, and professional development, it is important to know how to find, analyze, and interpret statistics and to share our findings in charts, tables, and text with our colleagues and others. We need to be able to teach the concepts of finding and analyzing statistical information to our students and patrons. Finally, an understanding of statistics is important to be able to participate in the scholarly conversations of our profession and help to build its knowledge base while developing our own. This is why a knowledge of statistics is important for us to have.

Statistical literacy as defined by Katherin K. Wallman, a former president of the American Statistical Association, is "the ability to understand and critically evaluate statistical results that permeate our daily lives—coupled with the ability to appreciate the contributions that statistical thinking can make in public and private, professional and personal decisions" (1993, 1). This definition implies that there is a base level of knowledge that will allow you to understand statistics as you encounter them in your everyday life.

Merriam-Webster defines statistics as, "a branch of mathematics dealing with the collection, analysis, interpretation, and presentation of masses of numerical data" ("Statistics" 2023). The *McGraw-Hill Dictionary of Scientific and Technical Terms* tells us that information is "data which has been recorded, classified, organized, related, or interpreted within a framework so that meaning emerges" ("Information" 2003). We analyze and interpret data to turn it into illuminating and actionable information.

For the purposes of this book, we will rename the definition of statistical literacy as a definition of "statistical information literacy," or the ability to understand, evaluate, and communicate statistical information. We will change the definition of statistics slightly to read: the collection, analysis, interpretation, and presentation of data. We will call this "statistical literacy." One of the primary goals of this text is to help you understand and do statistical analyses. We want you to have both statistical information literacy and statistical literacy skills. Developing your statistical literacy skills will improve your statistical information literacy abilities.

Terminology of Statistics

We will begin our discussion of statistics by looking at the concepts that impact the validity of research projects. A few of these concepts can be dealt with prior to data analysis, and others are a result of that analysis. These concepts are not inferential statistical tests, but they have a powerful impact on the outcomes of those tests.

Type I and Type II Errors

We will begin by talking about a difficult concept: errors. There are two types of errors. A Type I error is denoted by the Greek letter alpha, α. In a Type I error, the researcher mistakenly accepts the results of the alternative hypotheses as true when they are not. They have rejected the null hypothesis when in fact they should have accepted it as true. This type of error is also referred to as a false positive.

For statistical testing, we set a value of α that we are willing to accept. We set this value before we begin our research. In social sciences, we usually set a value for α of .05 thanks to the work of R. A. Fisher (Minitab Blog Editor 2012). This is called the significance level. By using a significance level of .05 we are saying that we will accept a 5 percent chance that the results represent a Type I error. We use α when we examine the significance of our test results.

A Type II error is denoted by the Greek letter beta, β. A Type II error returns a false negative. This is where the researcher accepts the null hypothesis as true, when in fact it is false. The researcher missed the fact that the alternative hypothesis, the one they want to show is true, is indeed true or positive.

The power of a research project is related to the possibility of committing a Type II error. Power is calculated by subtracting β from 1. Jacob Cohen suggests a power of .80 for general use. He suggests that anything smaller would "incur too great a risk of a Type II error" while anything larger would increase the sample size to an extent that likely exceeds the investigator's resources (1992, 156).

While both error types are serious, a Type I error is considered more problematic than a Type II error. Byrne illustrates this point with a hypothetical drug trial (2007).

A Type II error means you think your drug did not work when it did, but a Type I error would mean that you think your drug worked when it did not.

Significance

We have likely heard of the concept of statistical significance and the letter that represents it, p. Statistical significance is an indication that the results we got were not likely by chance and that there may be some meaning or value to the relationship we found between the variables in our research study. We know that the p-value needs to be low to indicate a statistically significant result from a test. What exactly is p? The p-value is the probability value, and it is calculated by the statistical test that you choose to run. It shows you how likely you are to get similar results if you run the same test again. It assumes that the null hypothesis is true.

The p-value is a number between 0 and 1. When we talk about the p-value, we talk in terms of percentages. If the p-value is .10, we say there is a 10 percent possibility that the results could happen by chance. We set the p-value as less than the significance level, the α we want to see. Typically, $p < .05$. This means there is a less-than 5 percent probability that the results happened by chance, and this is enough evidence to reject the null hypothesis and accept the alternative hypothesis. For exploratory research, a $p < .10$ is acceptable (Schumm 2010). For some research, a lower p-value will be required, as with drug testing. If the statistical test you used for your research returns a p-value of less than .05, we say the results are statistically significant. Your p-value should always be reported, and in cases where it is around .05, your readers can determine how to interpret your results.

Practical Significance

You created a research project, gathered your statistics, and ran your analysis. It was a lot of hard work. Your results indicate a strong statistical significance. The p-value is much less than .05. You are rightly excited. You report your findings to a colleague, and she just shrugs and says she is sorry you didn't find anything. What just happened? What does she mean?

Beyond the p-value, we need to make sure our results have *practical* significance. In your experiment, group A received special test instructions and group B did not. Group A had a mean score of 88, while group B had a mean score of 86 out of 100. Is this enough to be considered practically significant? If the difference in the means was 20 points, 88 versus 86, then there is no question that your results are both statistically and practically significant. If the mean scores were 88.2 and

88, then clearly you have only a statistically significant result, and not one that is practically significant.

Your 2-point difference is statistically significant, but is it practically so? Does it make that much of a real-world difference? What time, effort, and costs went into achieving that increase? Would something else cause the same result? Use your common sense in thinking about the results you achieved and be sure to talk about the practical aspect of those results in your analysis.

Sample

We talked about populations in Chapter 5. To review, a population is every member of a specified group, and the number of people in that group is denoted by the letter N. The population of your study could be all the freshmen at your high school or your university. If the population is large, we work with a sample—a smaller, more manageable number of people who represent the larger population. A sample is usually denoted by the letter "n." However, in psychology, N is used to denote the entire sample size or number of cases in your statistical analysis. That is everyone you sampled in every group, while n is used to represent the sample size or number of cases of a subgroup of a sample.

There are two primary ways to generate a sample. The first is called probability sampling. There are a few subtypes of probability sampling. In each type, every member of the population must have an equal chance of being selected to participate in the research study. Random sampling is the best-known type of probability sampling. In random sampling, you pick from every member of the population at random until you have enough participants. Stratified random sampling adds another consideration to the mix. In this case, you make sure that you have enough participants in a specified subcategory to match the population. If library card holders at your public library are 62 percent female, you may want to use stratified sampling to ensure that your participants are also 62 percent female. You do not want your participants to be 62 percent male, because that would not reflect your population and may skew your results.

Non-probability sampling is the second type of sampling. It is sampling that is not probabilistic in nature. Convenience sampling is a very common method. You use people who are convenient or easy to access. For example, your sample may consist of those who volunteered to participate in your study. You compile information from your survey based on those who responded to the link on your library's homepage. Snowball sampling is when you ask a participant if they know of anyone who may be interested in participating in your study. You contact those people, ask them to recommend others for the study, and so on. This can be labor-intensive. Quota sampling is similar to stratified sampling. You want to find enough people with a certain characteristic to meet the number you need for your research, but you use nonprobability sampling techniques to find them. For example, you are asking men in different age groups about their library usage. You have enough men in all your categories except one. So, you approach male library users and ask them if they are between the ages of thirty-five and fifty, and if so, would they participate in a survey? You do this just enough times to meet your quota.

In general, you need to use probability sampling to draw inferences about the population from the sample. If you sample enough freshmen to represent the population of freshmen at your school, you want to be able to say that your results represent all freshmen. Non-probability sampling introduces bias and reduces the validity of your results. It is best used for qualitative research ("Nonprobability Sampling" 2022).

Power Analysis

A power analysis is one way to calculate a sample size given a significance level, α, an effect size, and a power level. You can use it to calculate any one value given the other three. Another way to use it would be to calculate the effect size given a specific sample size, significance level, and power level. In other words, there is a relationship between each of these four elements. A change to one leads to changes in the others. If you need to adjust your significance level to α = .10 for a preliminary study, then your sample size can be smaller to find the same effect size.

There is an excellent free statistical power program from the University of Dusseldorf called G*Power (https://www.psychologie.hhu.de/arbeitsgruppen/allgemeine-psychologie-und-arbeitspsychologie/gpower.html) that will take you through variations of power calculations based on the statistical test you intend to use, like the *t*-test differences between independent means. You can find the sample size you need given the other three parameters, or you can find the effect size you will achieve. It also has a post hoc test, that shows you the power level of your research based on the sample size you had, the α you used, and the effect size you achieved ("G*Power" 2023). It can do power calculations for multiple statistical tests. G*Power is available for MacOS and Windows.

There is a module available for jamovi that will do power calculations but only for *t*-tests. jamovi's functionality can be extended by adding modules to its basic functionality. It is easy to add a module. With the Analysis tab selected, click on the plus icon on the top, left-hand side of the screen, then select "jamovi library" (Figure 6.1).

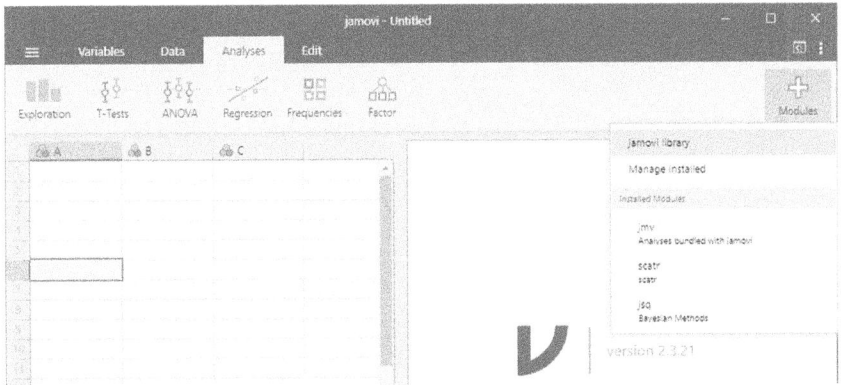

Figure 6.1 *Selecting the Modules Icon and proceeding to the jamovi Library of Add-on Modules.*
Source: jamovi.

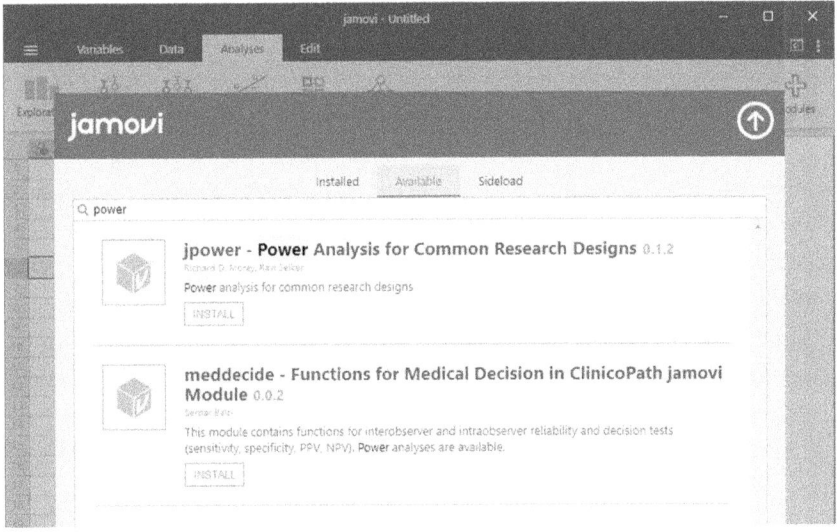

Figure 6.2 *A Search for "power" in the Add-on Modules of jamovi.*
Source: jamovi.

You can scroll through the list of modules that appear or search for a specific module, like the power analysis one (Figure 6.2).

In Figure 6.3, you can see that the power module is now available on the Analyses tab.

As your statistical needs change and grow, you can add other modules to further the abilities of jamovi. There is even a module that allows you to run R code inside of jamovi.

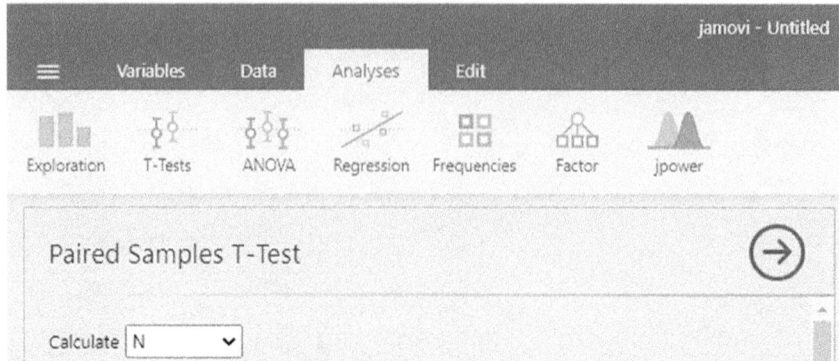

Figure 6.3 *Power analysis added to jamovi.*
Source: jamovi.

Sample Size

Sample size is an easy concept in the abstract. The larger your sample size, the greater the ability of statistical tests to find significant results, and the more likely your results will be normally distributed (Byrne 2007). The smaller your sample size, the less likely you are to find significant relationships. Sample size impacts the amount of work and costs associated with doing your research. Sample size, potential *p*-values, effect size, and the statistical power of your research are all intertwined (Cohen 1992). Changes to one affects all the others.

If you want to make inferences from a sample about the whole population, then you need to pay close attention to your sample size to ensure that your sample is large enough to accurately represent the population. There are tables and sample size calculators that will help. They use terminology that we have not introduced yet. Confidence level is the first important term. It is calculated by subtracting your α value from 1. In social science, we often set our α, or significance level, at .05, meaning that our results have a 5 percent possibility of falsely rejecting the null hypothesis. This would be a Type I error. Our confidence level would be 95 percent, meaning that 95 percent of the time our mean for our sample would be true of the population. The margin of error is frequently set at 5 percent which means it can be confused for α. However, the margin of error is not about Type I errors. It refines our confidence level and gives a range, the plus or minus 5 percent, which is called the confidence interval. If we have a survey with a 95 percent confidence level and a margin of error of 5 percent, this means that 95 times out of 100, we will find a mean within the confidence interval that is representative of the true population mean. If we ran a survey at those levels that found that 82 percent of students think information literacy is important, then rerunning the survey, we should see results between 77 percent and 87 percent 95 times out of 100.

If your school has 500 freshmen, $N = 500$, and if you want to sample them with a 95 percent confidence level and a margin of error of 5 percent, then you will need 217–18 results in order to represent all of the freshmen, or $n = 217$. The difference between the sample size is due to differences in rounding between the tables and calculators. You can find a simple sample size table that assumes a 95 percent confidence level and 5 percent margin of error at the University of Connecticut (https://researchbasics.education.uconn.edu/sample-size) (Siegle 2015). Another table provides sample sizes with different confidence levels and margins of error (https://www.research-advisors.com/tools/SampleSize.htm) ("Sample Size Table" 2006). Survey Monkey (https://www.surveymonkey.com/mp/sample-size-calculator) and Qualtrics (https://www.qualtrics.com/blog/calculating-sample-size) both provide sample size calculators that allow you to pick the confidence level and margin of error you want to use ("Sample Size Calculator: Understanding Sample Sizes" 2023, Qualtrics 2022).

These calculators and tables complement statistical power calculators. They tell you how many people you need to sample to represent the whole population, while a power analysis will tell you how many people you need to participate in your research to find a particular effect size.

Effect Size

Effect size is the strength of the association between variables or the magnitude of the change made by a treatment. We estimate the effect size we think we will see in our power analysis, and we determine the effect size we found through our statistical analysis of our research. Effect size is usually a number between 0 and 1. It can be a negative number that indicates the direction of the relationship. Cohen defined three general effect sizes—small, medium, and large. He defined a medium effect as one that is visible "to the naked eye of a careful observer" (1992, 156). Small is set at nontrivial, but significantly smaller than medium and closer to 0, and large is set at the same distance from medium as small, but closer to 1.

The effect size is different depending on the statistical test you are using. For a *t*-test, small, medium, and large effects are represented by the values .20, .50, and .80, respectively, and in this case, the test is called Cohen's *d*. For a correlation study, the numbers are .10, .30, and .50. You can find values of effect sizes from sources like Wikipedia and SPSS (Wikipedia contributors 2022; "Effect Size in Statistics—The Ultimate Guide" 2023). The SPSS site contains a link to a Google Sheets file that has a nice list of effect sizes (https://docs.google.com/spreadsheets/d/1dqbPqj3VfiHC3oZE

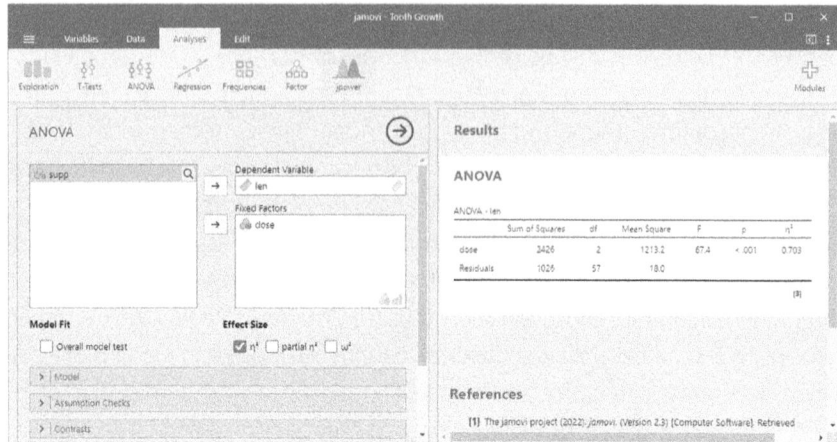

Figure 6.4 *An ANOVA analysis with effect size denoted by eta-squared, η^2.*
Source: jamovi.

4azLypiFOQaeoj9HQ8Z5yjOvybs). Statistical tests in jamovi often have a check box to include the calculated effect size in your results (Figure 6.4).

In some instances, you need to know the name of the additional test you need to apply to get the effect size data. For example, when running a correlation test, you want to make sure that Pearson is checked under the label "Correlation Coefficients." This will give you the effect size for correlations known as Pearson's *r*. In Figure 6.5, note that the results show both a positive and negative correlation.

Your sample size, significance level, power level, and effect size should all be included in your research report or paper. Reporting your effect size "enhances the presentation" of your findings and should be included along with your significance level (Olejnik and Algina 2003, 434). This is part of the statistical information you need to report so that those who read your information can understand the basic parameters of your research project. It will help them consider the generalizability of your research. You may report the power level and effect size you hope to see and what you actually achieved. We will talk about reporting results from statistical tests in the next chapter.

Concerns for Generalizability of Research

One of the goals of research is to uncover phenomena that are bigger than the scope of our research project. We study a sample to draw conclusions about the population as a whole. This is generalizability. A study may allow one to

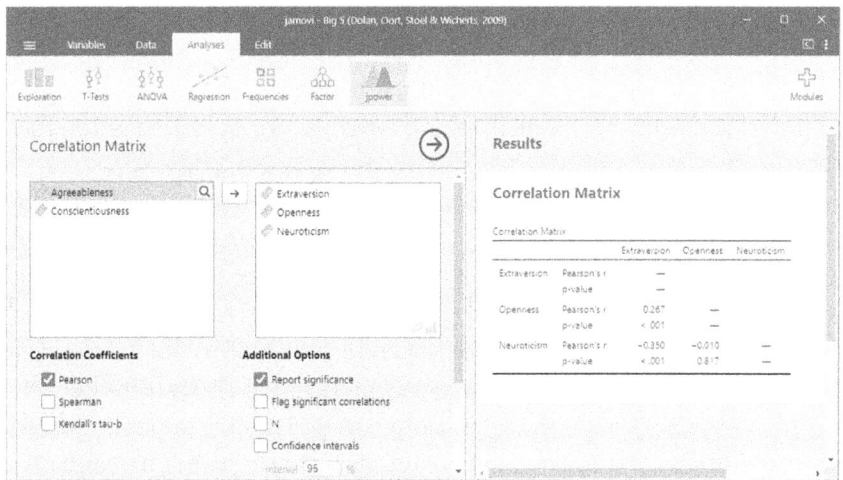

Figure 6.5 *Pearson's r showing the effect size of a correlation from a correlation matrix. Source: jamovi.*

infer information about all of the freshmen on a particular campus. With a good sample size and strong methodology, the results may be applicable to other similar colleges.

Can the results be applied to any college freshmen anywhere in the country? If the study was done at a rural, regional state university with open enrollment, would it apply to a private, urban college with high admission standards? It depends on what was being examined in the research. What kinds of behaviors, knowledge, or skills were being studied? The researcher would need to carefully describe the context of the research. Who are their students? Where do they come from? What is the college like? This information will help readers decide if the same conclusion may be true for their institutions. More importantly, it will help readers decide if the methods, results, and recommended actions would work for them, and whether the the knowledge gained from this research is transferable to their situation and institution. Transferability is the "process of applying the results of research in one situation to other similar situations" (Barnes et al. 2005) and is accomplished by the readers. It can be done with any type of research, not just quantitative research. For example, a case study cannot be generalized. By its nature, it does not allow for statistical testing from which inferences can be drawn. However, readers of the study may find insights into behavior and actions that they can transfer to their situation.

A well-planned, executed, and documented research study provides both good generalizability and transferability. These factors are improved with larger sample sizes which "produce more reliable results with less margin of error" (Gray 2005, 26). Researchers need to ensure that the sample is unbiased and "truly representative" (Christensen 1988, 87) of the population. Random samples and random assignment improve reliability and avoid bias. Surveys advertised on your library website may lead to self-selection bias where the group who chose to answer does not represent the population because of nonprobability sampling. On the other side of the coin, a low response rate to research questions or surveys may cause nonresponse bias where the group who did not answer the questions would have answered very differently than those who did. A researcher needs to explain potential problems with the data and how problems like missing data were handled. This improves the transparency and external validity of the research.

External validity is another way of saying how well can the results be applied to other situations and contexts. Internal validity is the confidence the researcher has that their results are valid due to the test conducted. The external validity of a research project directly impacts the transferability of the results. External validity can be viewed as the "effective link between knowledge generation and knowledge utilization" (Ferguson 2004, 16). After all, another goal of research is to have others utilize the knowledge generated to make decisions about policies and practices.

We want our research to be used by others to inspire further research, to solve problems, and to improve practice. The best way to do this is to ensure that our research is done well, is transparent, and produces generalizable results.

Summary and Reflection

In this chapter, we examined statistics, statistical literacy, and statistical information literacy. How important do you think statistical information literacy is for librarians to have? How important is it for your students and patrons?

We discussed a few important statistical concepts, like Type I and Type II errors, the α and β that represent them. We also talked about significance. How are significance, Type I, and Type II errors important in research? Statistical and practical significance are important results we determine from our research. When is practical significance a more important consideration than statistical significance? If your research does not find any statistically significant results, should you consider not publishing it or presenting it?

Sample size is one of the most important aspects of research. It helps determine the generalizability of research results. How else does sample size impact research results? What is a power analysis, and what does it show?

Effect size shows the magnitude of the relationship between variables in a research project. What does that mean? Are effects all the same? When and how are they calculated?

Generalizability means that our sample represents the population being studied. It means we can make inferences from the sample to the population. What else helps make research generalizable? What is transferability and how is it related to generalizability?

Implementation

With your research project in mind, use a sample-size table or calculator to determine how many people you would need to participate in your research project to represent a specific population you serve. What sample size would you need if you increased the significance level?

Using power analysis software, determine the power of your research based on the first sample size you found. If you want the power to be .80, do you need to increase the sample size?

Vocabulary

Confidence level
Confidence interval
Confounding factors
Effect size
External validity
Generalizability
Internal validity
Interval
Margin of error (confidence interval)
Nominal
Nonprobability sampling
Ordinal
p
Population
Power
Practical significance

Probability sampling
Ratio
Sample
Significance level
Statistical information literacy
Statistical significance
Transferability
Type I error
Type II error
Validity

References

Barnes, Jeffery, Kerri Conrad, Christof Demont-Heinrich, Mary Graziano, Dawn Kowalski, Jamie Neufeld, Jen Zamora, and Mike Palmquist. 2005. "Understanding Generalizability and Transferability." Writing@CSU. https://writing.colostate.edu.

Byrne, Gillian. 2007. "A Statistical Primer: Understanding Descriptive and Inferential Statistics." *Evidence Based Library and Information Practice* 2, no. 1: 32. https://doi.org/10.18438/B8FW2H.

Christensen, J. O. 1988. "Use of Statistics by Librarians." *Journal of Library Administration* 9, no. 2: 85–90.

Cohen, Jacob. 1992. "A Power Primer." *Psychological Bulletin* 112, no. 1: 155–9.

"Effect Size in Statistics - The Ultimate Guide." 2023. https://www.spss-tutorials.com/effect-size/.

Ferguson, Linda. 2004. "External Validity, Generalizability, and Knowledge Utilization." *Journal of Nursing Scholarship: An Official Publication of Sigma Theta Tau International Honor Society of Nursing* 36, no. 1: 16–22. https://doi.org/10.1111/j.1547-5069.2004.04006.x.

"G*Power." 2023. University of Düsseldorf. https://www.psychologie.hhu.de/arbeitsgruppen/allgemeine-psychologie-und-arbeitspsychologie/gpower.

Gray, Ann S. 2005. "Data and Statistical Literacy for Librarians." *IASSIST Quarterly* 28, no. 2: 24. https://doi.org/10.29173/iq793.

"Information." 2003. In *McGraw-Hill Dictionary of Scientific and Technical Terms*, 6th ed. New York: McGraw-Hill.

Minitab Blog Editor. 2012. "Alphas, P-Values, and Confidence Intervals, Oh My!" *Minitab Blog* (blog). October 1. https://blog.minitab.com/en/alphas-p-values-confidence-intervals-oh-my.

"Nonprobability Sampling." 2022. In *Wikipedia*. https://en.wikipedia.org/w/index.php?title=Nonprobability_sampling&oldid=1097626745.

Olejnik, Stephen, and James Algina. 2003. "Generalized Eta and Omega Squared Statistics: Measures of Effect Size for Some Common Research Designs." *Psychological Methods* 8, no. 4: 434–47. https://doi.org/10.1037/1082-989X.8.4.434.

Park, Jung Mee. 2022. "Statistics Training in Library Science: Comparing Approaches in Library and Information Science to Sociology Graduate Programs." *Journal of Education for Library & Information Science* 63, no. 2: 216–30. https://doi.org/10.3138/jelis-2020-0080.

Qualtrics. 2022. "Sample Size Calculator & Complete Guide in 2022." Qualtrics. August 29. https://www.qualtrics.com/blog/calculating-sample-size/.

"Sample Size Calculator: Understanding Sample Sizes." 2023. SurveyMonkey. https://www.surveymonkey.com/mp/sample-size-calculator/.

"Sample Size Table." 2006. Research Advisors. 2006. https://www.research-advisors.com/tools/SampleSize.htm.

Schumm, Walter R. 2010. "Statistical Requirements for Properly Investigating a Null Hypothesis." *Psychological Reports* 107, no. 3: 953–71. https://doi.org/10.2466/02.03.17.21.PR0.107.6.953-971.

Siegle, Del. 2015. "Sample Size." *Educational Research Basics* (blog). May 22. https://researchbasics.education.uconn.edu/sample-size/.

"Statistics." 2023. In *Merriam-Webster Dictionary*. Merriam-Webster. https://www.merriam-webster.com/dictionary/statistics.

Wallman, Katherine K. 1993. "Enhancing Statistical Literacy: Enriching Our Society." *Journal of the American Statistical Association* 88, no. 421: 1–8. https://doi.org/10.1080/01621459.1993.10594283.

Wikipedia contributors. 2022. "Effect Size." In *Wikipedia*.https://en.wikipedia.org/w/index.php?title=Effect_size&oldid=1116600227.

7 Running and Interpreting Statistical Tests in jamovi

> **Essential Questions**
>
> Use these questions to guide your reading:
> - Why is open software important to statistical analysis?
> - What are some of the standard statistical tests, and how are they run in jamovi?
> - How are the results of the statistical tests interpreted and reported?

Introduction

In Chapters 5 and 6, we introduced some statistical concepts like descriptive statistics, *p*-values, and jamovi for statistical analysis. We mentioned some of the information that is important to report when writing the results of your research for others to learn from. This information laid the groundwork for the material of this chapter.

We will start this chapter with a brief look at statistical software and open software. Then we will use jamovi to run inferential statistical tests. As long as you are not a mathematician or statistician, you likely will not need to learn how to do statistics by hand when there are great tools that can handle the calculations for you. However, you do need to learn how to use these tools, specifically what tests to apply, and how to read the output. We will also discuss how the results of statistical tests should be reported.

A Brief Overview of Statistical Software

Statistical software has been around for a long time. Statistical Analysis System, better known as SAS, was developed at North Carolina State University in 1966 ("SAS Software" 2022). Statistical Package for the Social Sciences, known as SPSS, followed in 1968 ("SPSS" 2022). To use these programs, you would have been working on a mainframe computer and writing code to tell the computer what functions to apply to your data. Both of these programs are still around today. Both run on Windows, and SPSS runs on Macs. They have graphical user interfaces that make them much easier to use, with no programming required. You can use these programs to do sophisticated statistical analysis without having to know how to manually solve the complex underlying equations. The problem with this software is its cost and licensing which makes research outside of a university, where there may be a side-wide license, prohibitive.

Fortunately, this problem was addressed with free software. PSPP, which does not stand for anything but an inversion of SPSS, is an SPSS work-alike, freeware program that came out in 1997 ("PSPP—GNU Project—Free Software Foundation" 2020). As a freeware, the software is copyrighted, maintained, and controlled by its copyright holders, but it is free to download, use, and does not expire like a license agreement (Fisher 2022).

R is perhaps the biggest name in statistics programs right now. R is a statistical programming language that became a free, open-source software in 1995 ("R (Programming Language)" 2022). Open-source software shares its source code and can be modified and built upon by anyone (Midrack 2021). R has more than 18,500 user-contributed "packages," R terminology for extensions, that enable the software to perform new functions, as of August 2022 ("CRAN—Contributed Packages" n.d.). As a programming language, you need to write code to use R. Various levels of graphical interfaces have been developed for R.

JASP and jamovi use R as their foundation and provide a point-and-click graphical interfaces such as SPSS and PSPP (Muenchen 2019; "Jamovi: Stats. Open. Now." n.d.). Both are open-source software packages used in hundreds of institutions around the world (Draws 2018; "List of Universities Using Jamovi to Teach Stats" n.d.; "Jamovi" n.d.; Kermer 2022; "Jamovi Statistical Software" 2022). What makes these programs important is that they democratize statistical analysis, making analysis easier to do and affordable for all.

jamovi Basics

JASP (https://jasp-stats.org) and jamovi (https://www.jamovi.org) are very similar programs with a similar look and feel. They both run on multiple platforms, Windows, Mac, and Linux, and have an option to run in the cloud. Both have additional resources to help you use the program including user guides, books, and videos. JASP includes Bayesian statistical tests and a larger library of example files. You can add JASP's Bayesian tests to jamovi by adding the jsq module to jamovi. The biggest difference between the two programs is that in JASP the data is stored in a spreadsheet and then imported into the program. Any editing of the information needs to be done in the spreadsheet. Jamovi supports a built-in spreadsheet where you can type in and edit the data you want the program to process (see Figure 7.1). This feature makes jamovi easier to use.

Once jamovi is installed (https://www.jamovi.org/download.html), you can begin entering data in the spreadsheet as illustrated in Figure 7.2, or you can directly open Excel, LibreOffice Calc, or, of course, jamovi omv files. Using the Special Import found by clicking on the collapsed menu icon, better known as the hamburger button ("Hamburger Button" 2023), will allow you to import files in many other formats including SAS, SPSS, JASP, and csv. If you enter data, you

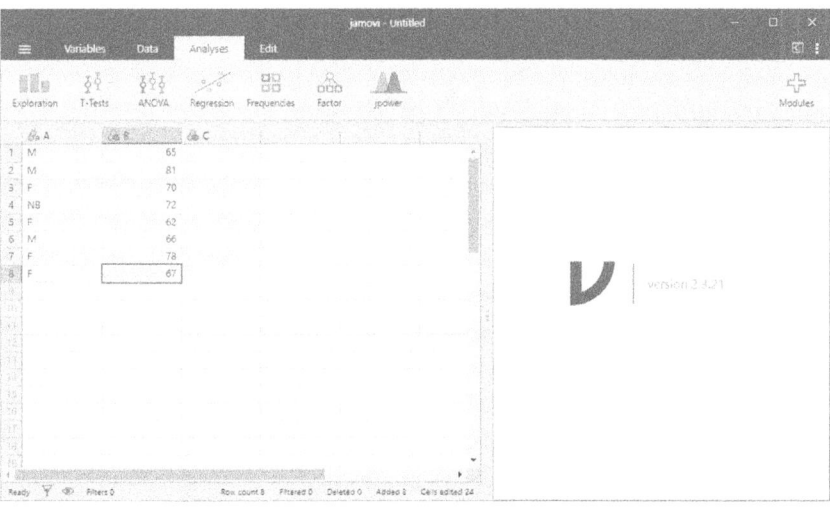

Figure 7.1 *Entering data into jamovi.*

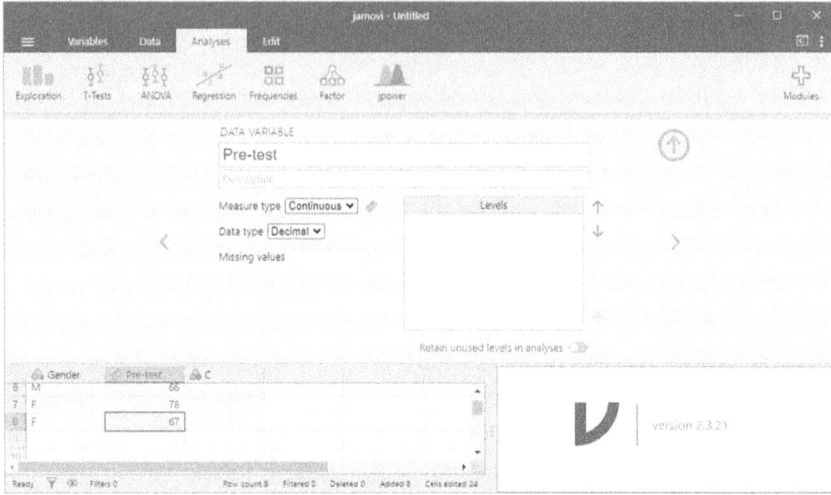

Figure 7.2 *Changing the name, measure type, and data type.*

need to select the column name by double-clicking on it to name your variables. From this screen, you also select the measure type of either nominal, ordinal, continuous, or ID. You also select the data type from this screen, which is either integer, decimal, or text. When importing a file, jamovi will make these decisions for you based on the type of data it finds. With your data entered or imported, you are ready to begin running statistical analyses.

Inferential Statistics with jamovi

The *t*-test is a suite of tests designed to compare means. Means do not have to be test scores but can be any average, like height, average number of print or audio books checked out, or average attendance at workshops. There are three *t*-tests, and they are slightly different in how the test is applied. The *t*-tests work well with small sample sizes. The tests are selected from the "T-Tests" menu as seen in Figure 7.3.

One Sample T-Test

The first statistical test we will talk about is the one-sample *t*-test in which a mean from one group, the sample, is compared to a previously defined mean. This mean could come from a national average test score, the average test score students achieved in the previous semester, or elsewhere. The one-sample *t*-test requires

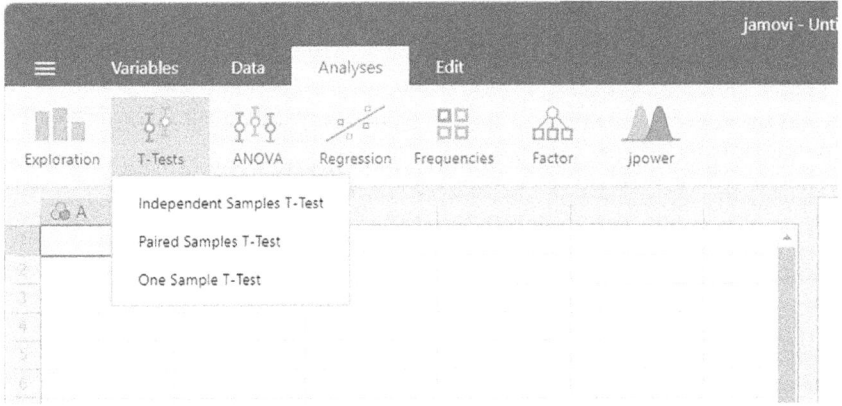

Figure 7.3 T-tests in jamovi.

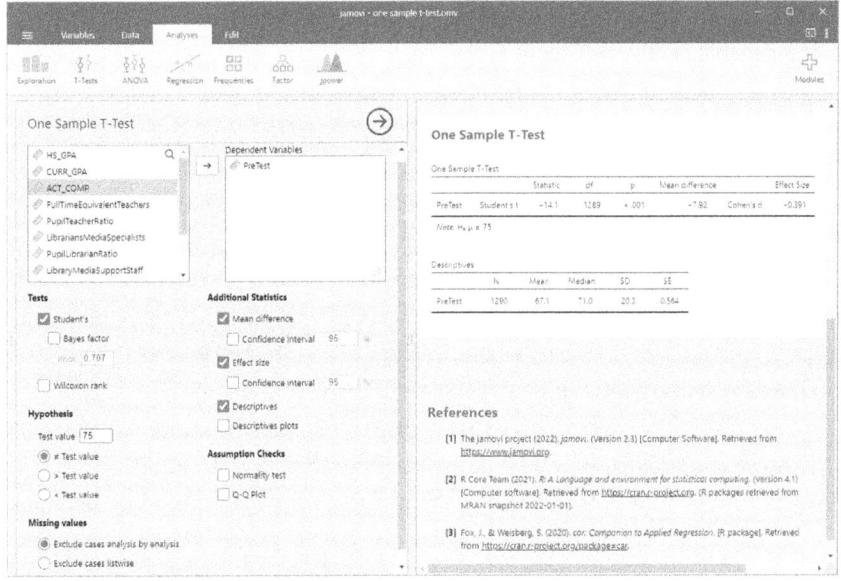

Figure 7.4 One sample t-test.

numeric scale data. Numeric data is interval or ratio data that jamovi puts into the category of continuous data. This is a parametric test. Parametric tests assume that the data will be normally distributed (Connaway and Powell 2010). However, this test is also robust and can handle violations of that assumption (Cronk 2004). To move a variable from the list on the left-hand side into the Dependent Variables box on the right-hand side, you can select it and click on the arrow, double-click on it, or drag it. In Figure 7.4, you can see that PreTest has been moved to the

Dependent Variables box. Note that two of the variables in the left-hand column are grayed out. The variables are of the wrong type to be used in a *t*-test and are not selectable.

Under "Tests," "student's" was already selected. In "Additional Statistics," "mean difference," "effect size," and "descriptives" were selected. The mean difference subtracts the test value from the class mean (65.1 − 75 = −9.91). The effect size gives Cohen's *d*, which is .507 indicating a medium effect. By having a "descriptives" selection within the specific test, descriptive statistics do not have to be run separately before the analysis. The descriptive statistics you receive here are not as complete as what you get from running them from the exploration menu, but it does give the number of cases in the sample and the mean and median values along with the standard deviation. The standard deviation, or *SD*, is 19.6. You will need to judge whether the standard deviation is a large value or not, given the measurement scale you are using. In this case, a nearly 20-point swing on a 100-point scale around a mean score of about 65 is large. It indicates that there was a lot of variability in the test scores.

The Test Value of 75 had to be input to represent the value the class is being compared with. The Normality test, a check to see if your data is normally distributed, that jamovi uses is the Shapiro–Wilk test. Because of the large number of people in this sample, a normality test is not needed, but if the sample were small, twenty or fewer according to one source (van der Berg 2023) or fifty or fewer according to another source (Stephanie 2022), then the Shapiro–Wilk test should be used, and the Normality test box should be checked. You can select the Q-Q plot and visually inspect your data for normality when dealing with larger sample sizes.

The last section on the analysis screen is "missing values." The option for "Exclude cases analysis by analysis" is checked by default. This option maximizes the use of your data. If you are examining more than one variable and a given case, or row, in your data is missing one of those variables, the other variables will still be used. The other option is "Exclude cases listwise." This will eliminate the whole case or row of data if one variable you are using is missing. For example, if you are analyzing five variables for 100 people, all 100 cases may be used if you exclude cases by analysis even though there is missing data in many of the cases. If you exclude data listwise, and only fifty participants have answers to all five of the variables, then only those fifty cases will be used in the analysis.

Reading the results of the one-sample *t*-test from the right-hand side of the screen, we see that our *p*-value is less than .001. It is statistically significant, and it means we have enough evidence to reject the null hypothesis and accept the alternative hypothesis as being more probable. Cohen's *d* is about −.5, which is a medium-sized effect with the minus sign showing that the group mean is less than the test value, and the difference between the means is about 10 points on a 100-point scale. These indicate that we have also found a practically significant difference in means. The *t*-statistic is −6.47. The higher the absolute value of the *t*-statistic, the greater the difference in means and the more evidence there is to reject the null hypothesis. There is no set scale for *t*-values. They are dependent on the degrees of freedom, df, in the analysis. The df in our test is 162. You can look at a *t*-distribution table for your df and α and find a critical value. If your *t*-statistic is greater than that value, you have a meaningful analysis.

Degrees of freedom can be a confusing concept in statistics. In our example, we have 162 df and our sample size is 163. The degrees of freedom in this case is our sample size, *n*, minus 1, or 162 df. The degrees of freedom are the "number of remaining free choices you have after something has been decided" (Donnelly 2007, 126). In other words, 162 test scores can take any value, but the 163 has to take on a specific value that will make the mean test score, or something that has been decided, equal 65.1.

When reporting the results of your analysis in writing, you need to provide "sufficient information to help readers fully understand the analyses conducted and possible alternative explanations for the outcomes of those analyses" (American Psychological Association 2019, 88). The *APA Publication Manual* and other books provide examples of how to report the results of statistical tests (American Psychological Association 2019; Cronk 2004; Goss-Sampson 2019). The reporting is very similar between sources, with Cronk and Goss-Sampson reporting test values as parenthetical information and APA reporting those values as non-parenthetical. With values rounded to two decimal places, this is how the results can be reported:

> A one sample *t* test found a significant difference between the mean test score and the test value of 75 ($t(162) = -6.47$, $p < .001$, $d = .51$). The sample mean of 65.1 ($SD = 19.6$) was significantly less than the test value.

The APA version would look like:

> ... and the test value of 75, $t(162) = -6.47$, $p < .001$, $d = .51$. The sample mean of 65.1 ($SD = 19.6$) was significantly less than the test value.

Independent Samples T-Test

In the independent samples *t*-test, the same test is given to two independent groups of people. The test assumes that the two groups are equal and will have

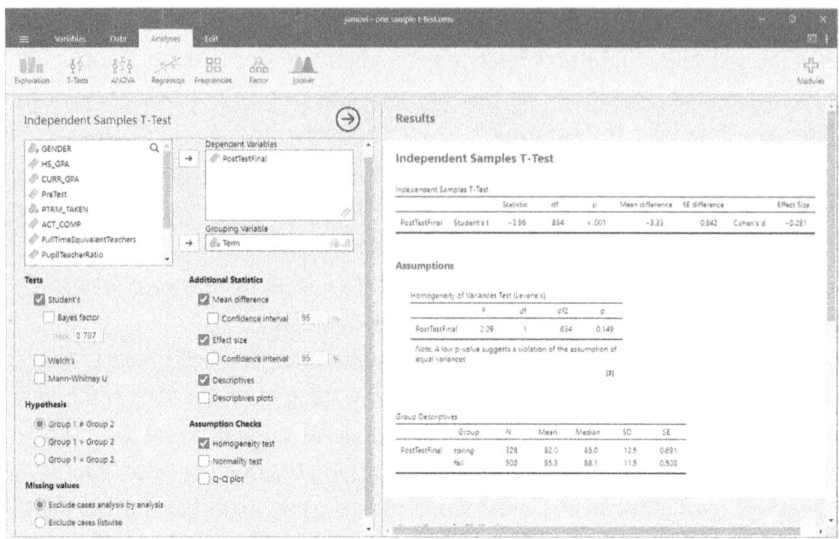

Figure 7.5 *Independent samples* t-*test.*

equal variance. This is a robust parametric test. Some variation from the normal distribution will not affect the results. With a two-group design, one group can be the control while the other is the experimental group. You can also compare groups based on many other factors, such as sex, time of day, and age. The dependent variable needs to be continuous, and the grouping variable needs to be nominal or ordinal. The icons for those data types are in the Grouping Variable box, and you can see the variables from the list of variables that have the appropriate icons. A grouping variable is how you separate one group from another. In the example below, the grouping variable is the term, either fall or spring, that an information literacy class was taken (Figure 7.5).

In addition to the standard checks, "Mean difference," "Effect size," and "Homogeneity test" were selected. The test for homogeneity examined the two groups to see if the variability in each group was the same, and that the distribution of test scores was similar. The *p*-value of .149 is larger than the significance level of .05. In this case that means the distributions are similar. If the *p*-value had been less than .05, then the two groups have different distributions, and comparing the two would not yield valid results.

The *p*-value for the *t*-test is less than .001, meaning that a statistically significant difference was found between fall and spring students on the post-test. Cohen's *d*, .28, indicates a small effect size, and the 3.33-point difference in the means is a pretty small value. The grade for either test score is a B.

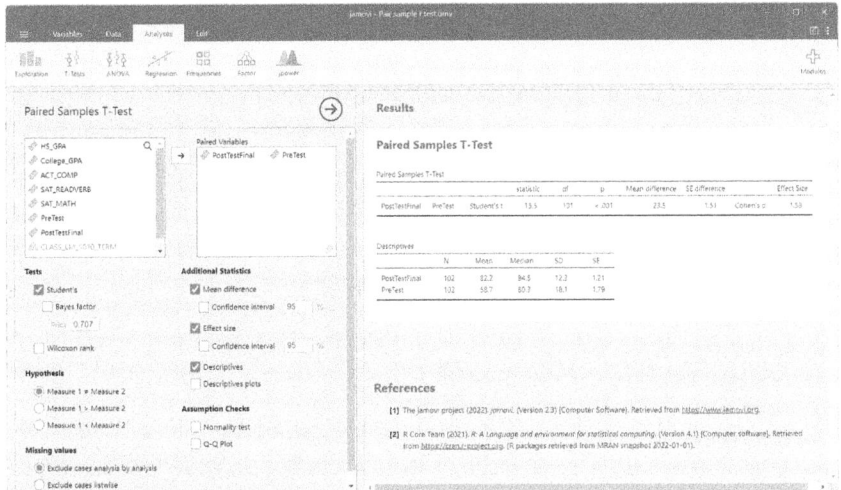

Figure 7.6 *Paired samples* t-*test.*

Here is how the results of the test can be reported:

An independent samples *t*-test found a statistically significant difference between the mean posttest score between students enrolled in information literacy classes in fall and spring semesters (*t*(834) = –3.96, *p* < .001, *d* = .28). The mean of the test score for students enrolled in fall (*M* = 85.3, *SD* = 11.5) was higher than students enrolled in spring (*M* = 82, *SD* = 12.5). However, this difference is small and not practically significant.

Paired Samples T-Test

The last *t*-test is the paired samples *t*-test (Figure 7.6). This test allows you to examine the effect of a treatment on one group. There is no control group. This is a parametric test, and it is fairly robust in dealing with violations of assumed normality. It needs two continuous data measures. This design is great for pre-test versus post-test comparisons.

For this test, pre-test and post-test scores were examined in an information literacy class to determine the level of information literacy skills students had at the beginning of class versus what they learned during the class.

The *t*-value is large at 15.5. The *p*-value is less than .001, indicating statistical significance. Cohen's *d* is 1.53, which is a very large effect size, and the mean difference of 23.5 also attests to the large size of the difference. An improvement in post-test scores is certainly expected. What is unexpected about these results were the low scores on the pre-test and the size of the improvement on the post-test.

Here is how the results of the test can be reported:

A paired samples *t*-test found a statistically significant difference between the mean pretest and mean posttest score of students enrolled in information literacy classes (l(101) = 15.5, $p < .001$, $d = 1.53$). The mean of the posttest ($M = 82.2$, $SD = 12.3$) was significantly larger than the pretest score ($M = 58.7$, $SD = 18.1$).

Chi-Square Test: Goodness of Fit

The chi-square tests, which can also be denoted using the Greek letter as X^2, are nonparametric tests, meaning that the data is not normally distributed, or it is not of interval or ratio variety. Nonparametric tests have less power than parametric tests to find significant differences. Larger sample sizes can overcome this issue. Interestingly, nonparametric tests can be used with smaller sample sizes (Connaway and Radford 2017), so be sure to take note of your *p*-values. In the case of chi-square, the test requires nominal or ordinal data, also known as categorical data.

The chi-square test comes in two forms: goodness of fit and test of association. The goodness of fit version compares the frequency of answers to theoretical, expected frequencies for those answers. The test assumes that there will be at least one expected answer per category with at least 80 percent of the categories needing to have expected frequencies of five or more. The chi-square test tells us only if there is a significant deviation or not from what we expected to see. It does not tell us about the strength of that deviation.

The test is located on the Frequencies menu, under the name of N outcomes: X^2 Goodness of fit. The test only takes one variable. The example in Figure 7.7 shows that Book Type was placed into the Variable window. The option "Expected counts" was checked in order to see how many items in each category were expected to be there. This number appears directly under the "Observed Count" in the test output. The "Expected Proportions" tab was open to show that the expected numbers do not have to be even across the categories and can be adjusted.

Our sample dataset looks at which type of book was checked out over a period of time: either print, ebook, or audio. The expected proportions were left at equal values. So, each type of book was expected to be checked out 36.3 times. The X^2 statistic is like the *t*-statistic in that meaning emerges when compared to critical values based on degrees of freedom and the α. As in the case of *t*-test, we know that the X^2 value is above the critical value. Larger values of X^2 are more likely to

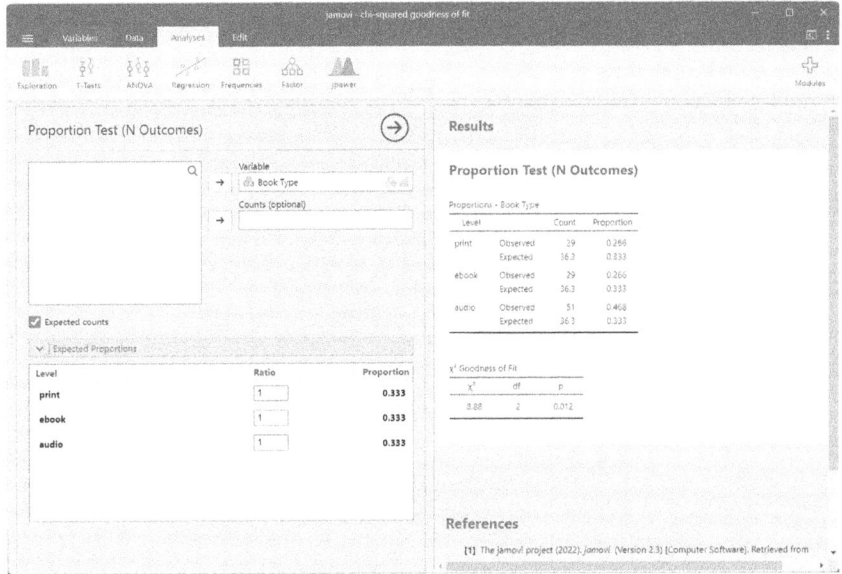

Figure 7.7 *Chi-square goodness of fit test.*

be above the critical value. Notice that there is no effect size test for goodness of fit. You are left to draw your own conclusions.

For example, if we change the Expected Proportions to reflect what we believe to be an accurate representation with Ratio for "print" left at 1, the Ratio for "ebooks" dropped down to .8 (we expect fewer checkouts for ebooks than print titles), and "audio" books increased to 2 (representing the highest checkout rate), the chi-square test does not generate a significant *p*-value. This non-significant result indicates that the items were checked out at about these new expected rates. Here is how the results of the test can be reported:

> A chi-square goodness of fit test was conducted to see if the three formats of books, print, ebook, and audio, checked out at the same rate. The results of the test found a significant difference ($X^2 (2) = 8.88, p = .012$), indicating that types of materials are not selected at even rates.

Chi-Square Test: Test of Association

The chi-square test of association, also known as the chi-square test of independence, examines two variables to see if there is a relationship among the variables or if they are independent from each other. The test of association is similar to the goodness of fit test, except that it uses two nominal or ordinal

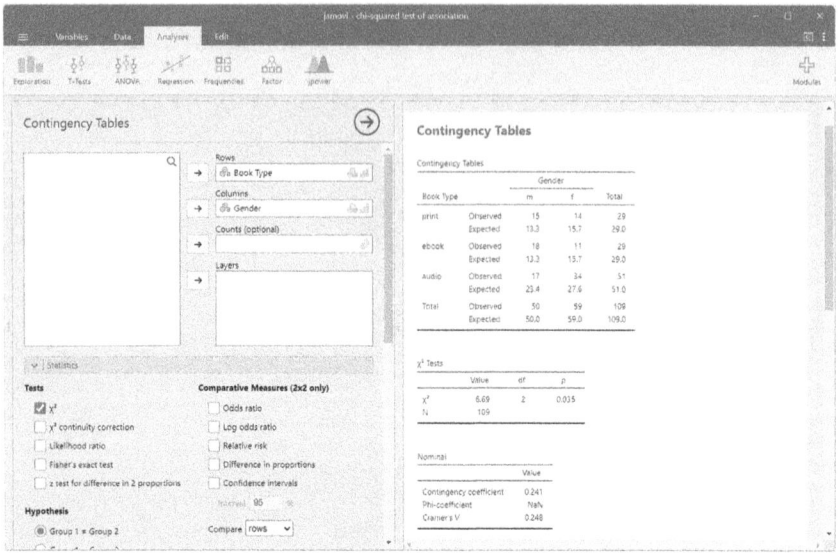

Figure 7.8 *Chi-square test of association showing variables.*

variables. Like the goodness of fit test, it is nonparametric and examines the frequencies of answers, comparing them to expected values. The test of association also assumes that there will be at least one expected answer per category with at least 80 percent of the categories needing to have expected frequencies of five or more answers.

The test is located on the "Frequencies" menu under the "Contingency Tables" banner and is listed as Independent Samples: X^2 test of association. In the example in Figure 7.8, the data has two nominal variables, "Book Type" and "Gender." "Book Type" was moved to "Rows," and "Gender" was moved to "Columns." The X^2 box is checked by default. The X^2 continuity correct is used with small samples when expecting that there will be categories with fewer than five entries. The Likelihood ratio is also used for small samples of less than thirty (Goss-Sampson 2019).

Further down the screen, but still under the "Statistics" options, we find "Nominal" and "Ordinal" options. Our example file used nominal data, so we will investigate these options first. The "Contingency coefficient" and "Phi and Cramer's V" are both measures of effect size. The contingency coefficient is used when you have five or more values in each variable. That means it should be used if you have a large table of data. The Phi coefficient has no value in our example. It only works with 2 by 2 tables. That leaves Cramer's V as our effect size. You will need to consult an effects size table. Find the row with your degrees of freedom and then check the values. Our .248 is a moderately strong association between the variables.

On the "Ordinal" side of the "Statistics" options, we see "Gamma," "Kendall's tau-b," and "Mantel–Haenszel." These are the effect size tests for ordinal data. Gamma is a standard test, but tends to give strong association values. Kendall's tau-b works with square tables, and Mantel–Haenszel is for 2 by 2 tables. The data in our example are nominal, so these options were not checked.

Under the "Cells" option, "Observed counts" and "Expected counts" are both checked. This allows us to see each of these values for all of the data. Percentages can be added by row, which allows us to see the percent of men versus women who checked out print books, for example. Percentages can also be added by column, allowing us to read down a column and see the percentages of men who checked out each book format. Finally, "Total" percentages can be added that show the percent of the total that each cell represents to both the row and the column. These options are illustrated in Figure 7.9.

The last option is "Plots," which will draw a bar chart. Bar charts are a useful visualization of your data, and a quick way to see the relationship that the chi-square test analyzed. You can control whether you want a stacked bar or side-by-side chart, whether you want the bars to represent counts or percentages, and finally which information you want on the X-axis (see Figure 7.10).

Here is how the results of the test can be reported:

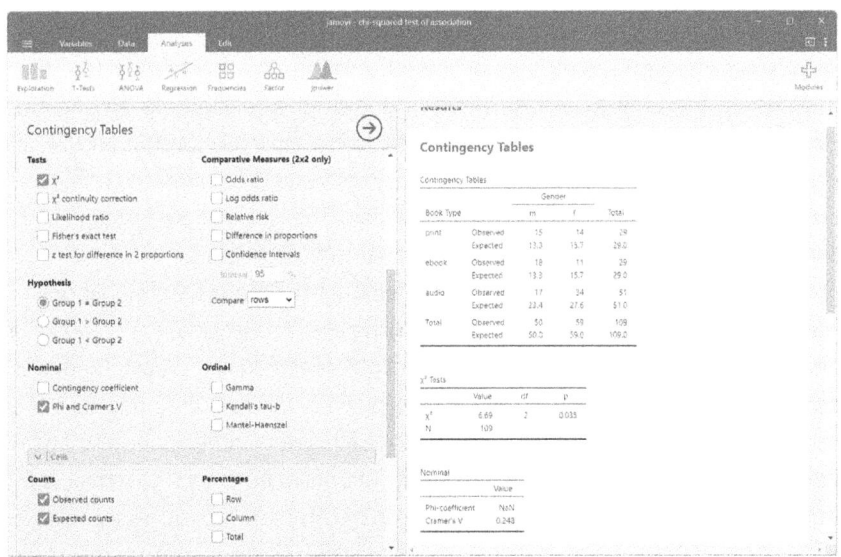

Figure 7.9 Chi-square test of association showing tests and cells options.

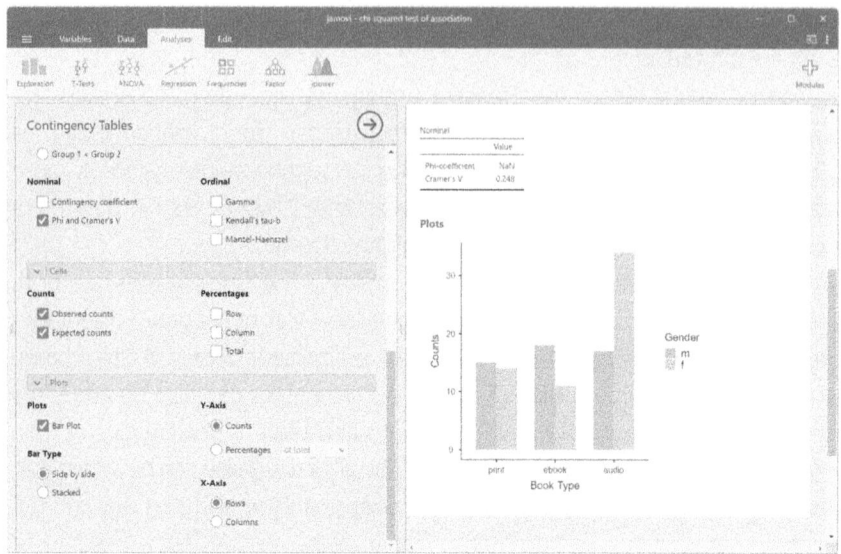

Figure 7.10 *Chi-square test of association showing the bar plot.*

A chi-square test of association was used to compare the frequency of circulation of print, ebooks, and audiobooks by gender. The test found a significant difference ($X^2(2) = 6.69$, $p = .035$) with ebooks and audiobooks accounting for the difference.

Correlations

Pearson's correlation coefficient, or just correlation, is a parametric test that is similar to the chi-square test in that it looks for a relationship among the variables. It needs continuous or ordinal data, with a linear relationship, and like all parametric tests, the data should be normally distributed. Spearman's correlation coefficient can be used with nonparametric data. The variables are tested in pairs and a correlation matrix is displayed with the results of the tests.

The example in Figure 7.11 looks at the amount of time students in an online class spent reading the course materials, taking exams (assessments) or working on the assignments, and the total number of points earned in the class. There was no need to check any of the boxes or radio buttons, the default settings are fine for this material. Two values are provided for each pair of correlations. The first is Pearson's *r*, which is a measure of effect size with between .1 and .3 as small, .3–.5 as moderate, and .5 and up as large. Pearson's *r* can have a positive or negative value. A positive value indicates that as one variable increases, so does the other. A negative value means that as one variable increases, the other decreases. The

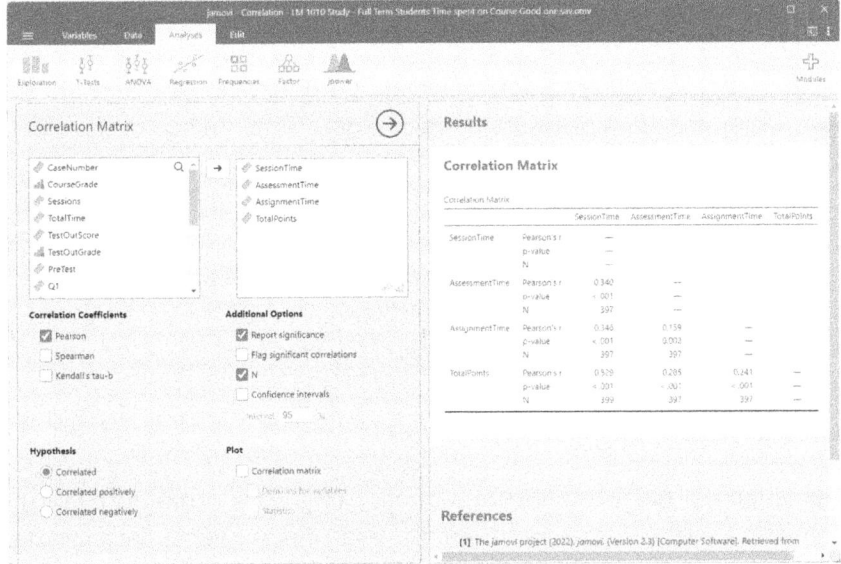

Figure 7.11 *Pearson's correlation coefficient.*

second value is the *p*-value, and as usual, values of less than .05 are considered statistically significant.

Half of the correlation matrix is left blank because it would repeat the information that is displayed. The dashes indicate where a row and column intersect with the same item. If we look at the "AssessmentTime" column, the first cell beneath it is where "AssessmentTime" intersects "SessionTime." This cell is left blank because this information is already in the "SessionTime" column. The second cell down contains dashes because this is where the two "AssessmentTimes" intersect. In the third cell down, we see where "AssessmentTime" intersects "AssignmentTime." Pearson's *r* is .159, which is a positive but weak correlation. The *p*-value is .002, meaning the small correlation is statistically significant. All of the correlations in this matrix are statistically significant and range in effect size from small to large. This is not surprising. It confirms that the more time spent on a task, the better students do on other tasks. The most interesting piece of information has a large effect size of .529 and shows that the more time students spend with the course materials, the better their overall score in the class.

If there were only a pair of items in our correlation, we would write the results like this:

> The correlation between SessionTime and TotalPoints (*r* (397) = .529, *p* < .001) found significant results with a large effect size.

Note that degrees of freedom for a correlation is $n - 2$. So, our degrees of freedom are 399 – 2, or 397.

Since we have multiple pairs of correlations, it is easier to include the correlation matrix table, and then talk about the results in general. Here is how the results of the test can be reported:

> A Pearson correlation examined the relationship between session time, assessment time, assignment time, and total points. All pairs were positively correlated and significant. The association between SessionTime and TotalPoints had the strongest correlations with a large r value of .529.

Simple Linear Regressions

Regression analyses follow from correlations nicely. While a correlation tells us if there is a relationship between variables, a regression gives us the means to predict an outcome based on that relationship. A simple linear regression has one dependent and one independent variable. The dependent variable should be continuous data, and it should be normally distributed. The independent variable, if using continuous data, is called a covariate, and it should be normally distributed as well. There should be a linear relationship between the variables as in a correlation analysis. Nominal variables can be used if they are dichotomous, having either a yes or a no value indicating the presence or absence of a quality.

Figure 7.12 shows that our dependent variable is "TotalPoints," and our covariate is "SessionTime." These are the two variables with the strongest effect size from our correlation analysis.

The only option applied to this analysis is under the "Model Fit" menu. "F test" from "Overall Model Test" was added to the R and R^2 from the "Fit Measures" as seen in Figure 7.13. The R statistic is the same as Pearson's r from the correlation analysis. The R^2 statistic indicates the strength of the relationship between the variables. It is read as a percentage. In our example, we would say that 28 percent of the variance in the dependent variable, total points earned in the class, can be explained by the variance in the independent variable, the amount of time spent with course materials. R^2 will be a value between 0 and 1, with 0 meaning that the model can never predict the outcome correctly and 1 meaning that the model is correct in predicting the outcome every time.

While R^2 tests the relationship, the F-test validates the model. In our example, the value of p is less than .001. This means that the F-test is significant, which in turn means that R^2 is significantly different from 0, and that the "correlation

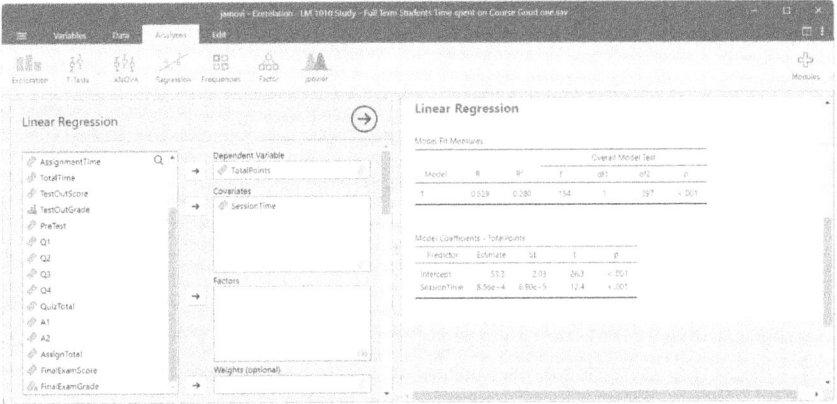

Figure 7.12 *Simple linear regression.*

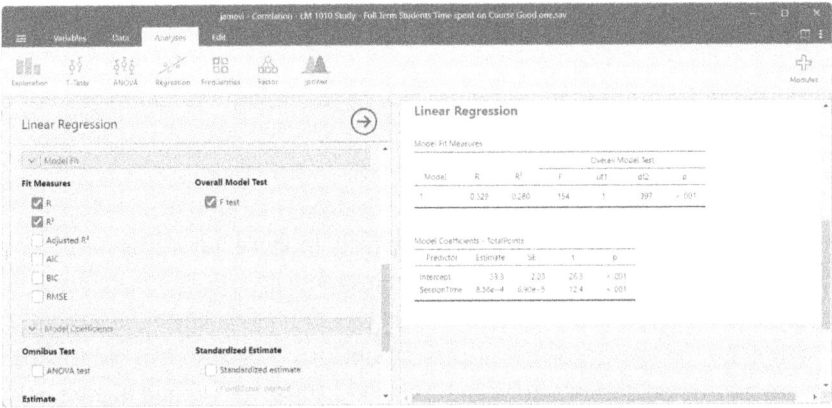

Figure 7.13 *F-test for simple linear regression.*

between the model and dependent variable is statistically significant" (Frost 2017, n.p.). For F statistics, the greater the value, the better.

The second part of the output is the Model Coefficients. The information here is used to build the predictive equation. The simple linear regression equations is:

$$y = c + (b * x)$$

The y represents the dependent variable. In our case, y represents the total points earned in the class. The c is a constant. Its value is taken from the "Intercept" row and the "Estimate" column. Our c is equal to 53.3. The b is the regression coefficient. Its value comes from the "SessionTime" row and the "Estimate" column. That value is 8.56e-4 which is $8.56*10^{-4}$, or 8.56*.0001 which equals .000856. The

x stands for session time which is measured in seconds. If we substitute a value for x like 6,000, meaning students spent an additional 100 minutes with course materials, we can solve the equation:

$$y = 53.3 + (.000856 * 6000), \text{ then } y = 5.14.$$

So, if students spend an additional 100 minutes going over the course materials, they can expect to see an improvement of 5.14 additional points in their total points for the class.

Here is how the results of the test could be reported if we had run the assumption checks and found no problems with our data. We will discuss the assumption checks in the next section on multiple linear regressions:

A simple linear regression shows that SessionTime is a significant predictor of TotalPoints ($F(1,397) = 154, p < .001$) with an R^2 of .28.

Additionally, the regression equation can be reported:

The fitted regression model is: TotalPoints = 53.3 + (.000856 * SessionTime).

Multiple Linear Regression

A multiple linear regression looks at the effects multiple influences have on a dependent variable. It is a simple linear regression with two or more covariates or factors. The dependent variable should be continuous and have a normal distribution. The independent variables should also have a normal distribution. The variables should be related to each other in a linear fashion, and there should be a homogeneity of variance, meaning the variance should be the same or similar. The independent variables, in this case also known as the predictor variables, should not be collinear. Collinearity is when variables are strongly correlated to each other. This strong correlation can "cause problems when evaluating the model" (Navarro and Foxcroft 2018, 310). The independent variables can also be dichotomous, nominal data.

Our multiple regression was run with a few additional checks: the "Adjusted R^2" and "F" test from the "Model Fit" menu and the "Standardized Estimate" from the "Model Coefficients" menu. The adjusted R^2 is an improved measure of the strength of the relationship. When there are multiple independent variables, R^2 tends to exaggerate the relationship. The adjusted R^2 compensates for that effect. It will increase in value if additional independent variables improve the model. It will decrease in value if additional variables decrease the predictive power of the model. The value of adjusted R^2 is always less than the value of R^2 ("Adjusted

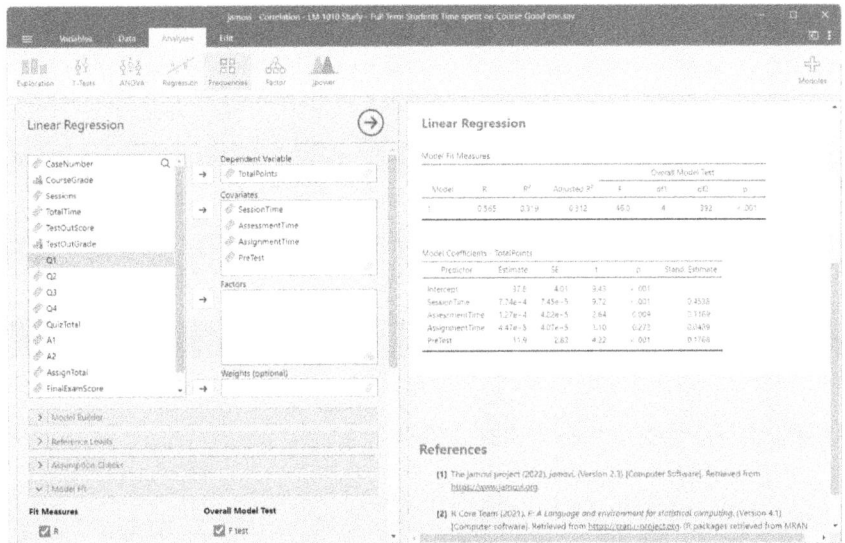

Figure 7.14 *Multiple linear regression analysis.*

R^2/Adjusted R-Squared: What Is It Used For?" 2023). The F-test indicates that our model works.

The standardized estimate is useful when the measures in the regression use different scales. Three of our measures use seconds, but one uses points. Using standardized estimates converts the measures to comparable values. The standardized estimate is listed in the "Model Coefficients" box of the output as seen in Figure 7.14. Another thing to note in that box is that each independent variable has a *p*-value. The value for "AssignmentTime" is greater than .05, meaning it is not significant.

There are ways that you can test the goodness of your model. First, you can simply put values in and take them out while watching what happens to the R^2 and adjusted R^2 values and the F-test value. Another method would be to add additional model tests to the analysis. Under the "Model Fit" menu, you can add "AIC" and "BIC" to the analysis. Both of these tests can help you select the best model. The lower the number, the better the model. Again, you can now add and remove variables while watching how AIC and BIC values change. The output of the regression with AIC and BIC are shown in Figure 7.15.

Another method is to use the "Model Builder" menu since one of our models is a subset of the other. Figure 7.16 illustrates how the Model Builder works. When first opening this menu, there is only Block 1, and it contains all the independent variables we are using in our regression. Select "Add New Block," and Block 2

Linear Regression

Model Fit Measures

Model	R	R²	Adjusted R²	AIC	BIC	Overall Model Test			
						F	df1	df2	p
1	0.565	0.319	0.312	3570	3594	46.0	4	392	< .001

Figure 7.15 *Multiple linear regression output with AIC and BIC values.*

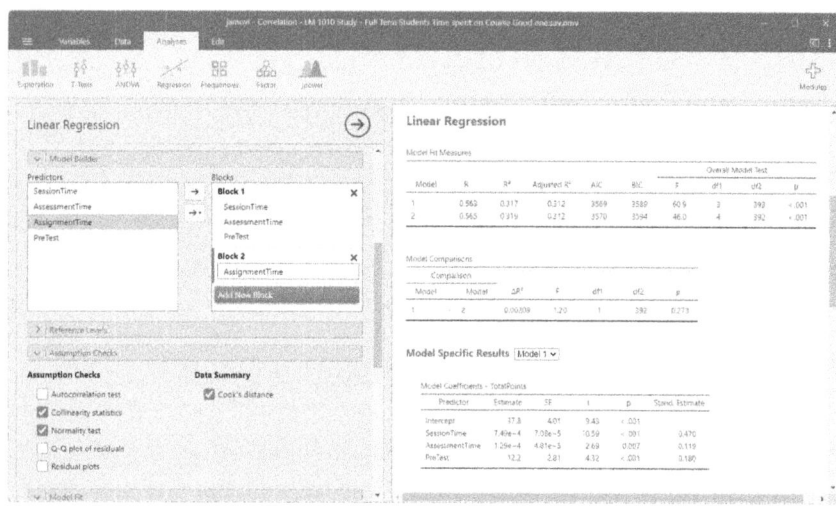

Figure 7.16 *Using Model Builder to test the fit of two models.*

appears. We think that "AssignmentTime" is a suspect variable, so we move it out of Block 1 and into Block 2. The output now shows the results of the regression using two models. Model 1 corresponds to Block 1, and Model 2 corresponds to Block 1 plus Block 2. We see that the AIC and BIC values are lower, and the F value is higher in Model 1 than in Model 2. This tells us that Model 1 is a better fit.

The output now gives us a "Model Specific Results" section, as seen in Figure 7.14, where we can choose to view either of the models evaluated and see the variables. We selected some options under the "Assumptions Check" menu to test how well our data works with the assumptions that regression analyses call for. We selected "Collinearity statistics," and "Normality test," as well as "Cook's distance" from the "Data Summary" list.

The "Autocorrelation test" from the "Assumption Checks" menu runs the Durbin–Watson test. This test checks the residual values for independence. The residuals should not be related to each other. If they are, this violates one of the assumptions that needs to be true in order for the regression analysis to produce good values. In Figure 7.15, the Durbin–Watson statistic is .711 and the *p*-value is less than .001. If the test is significant, as our *p* indicates, then there is autocorrelation of the residuals which is what we do not want. Also, you want to see the Durbin–Watson statistic with a value close to 2. Our data has failed this test.

The Collinearity statistics is a check of the collinearity, or multicollinearity, of the predictor variables. If these variables are highly correlated such that when one changes so does the other, then they are not providing independent values to the analysis (Zach 2019). This will have a negative impact on the model the regression produces. Collinearity statistics give two values to each of the predictor variables, a VIF and a Tolerance. If VIF values are greater than 1 and Tolerances are less than .2, then the model may be biased. If VIF values are greater than 10 and the Tolerance is less than .1, then the necessary assumptions have been "greatly violated" through collinearity of the variables (Goss-Sampson 2019, 75). As you can see in Figure 7.17, the VIF's in Model 1 are slightly larger than 1 and the Tolerances are greater than .2. Our collinearity should not be a problem.

The Normality test applies the Shapiro–Wilk test to see if the data are normally distributed, another assumption that needs to be met for the regression to work

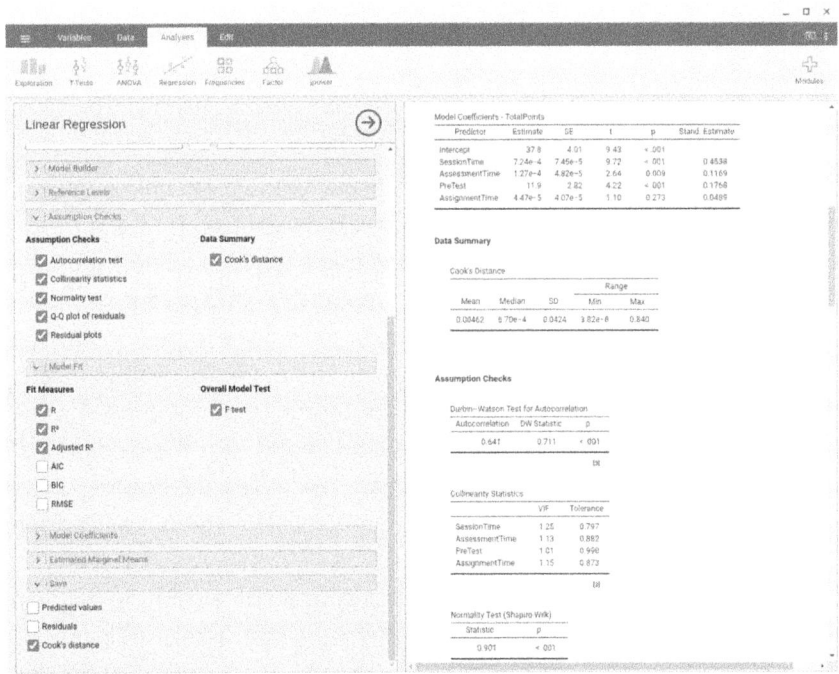

Figure 7.17 *Multiple regression with assumption checks applied.*

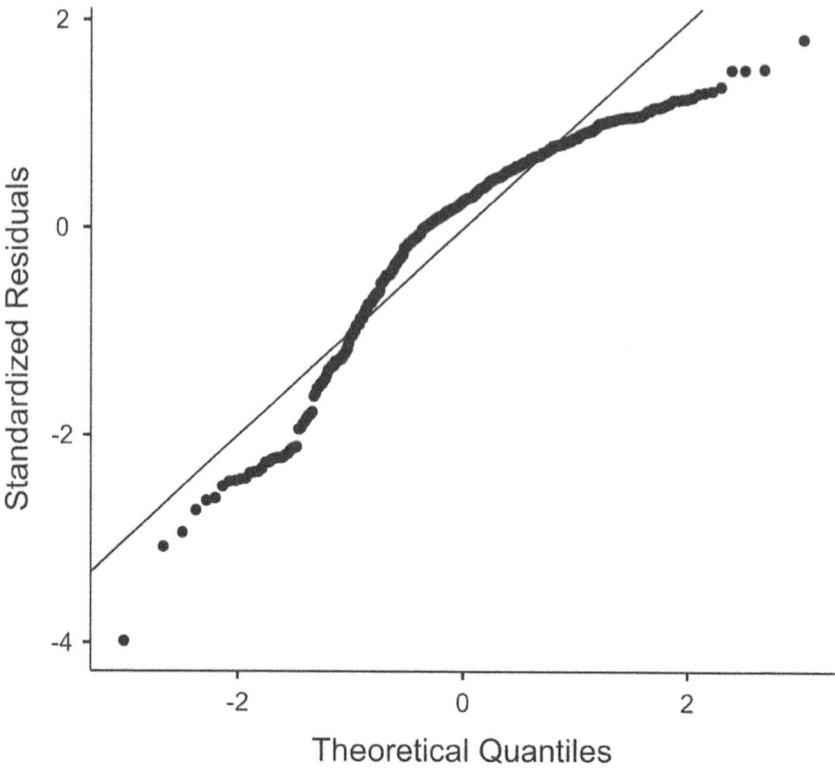

Figure 7.18 *Q-Q plot of multiple regression showing a poor fit.*

well. In this case, we want to see a *p*-value greater than .05. In our example, our *p*-value is less than .001. The data are not normally distributed.

Cook's distance is a measure of outliers that have high influence on the model. An outlier of this type can skew the equation and produce a model that is not accurate. Values between .5 and 1 may need to be investigated, because they may be causing problems with the regression. Values greater than 1 are highly influencing the results of the regression and need to be investigated as an outlier. Is there something wrong with the recording of the data? To check this, go to the "Save" menu and select the box for "Cook's distance." This will save the values to your spreadsheet where you can find and investigate them.

Our regression has passed some tests and failed others. Finally, you can generate plots and visually examine the data. Our Q-Q plot, as seen in Figure 7.18, is curved about the line it needs to follow. This shows a violation of the assumption of linearity.

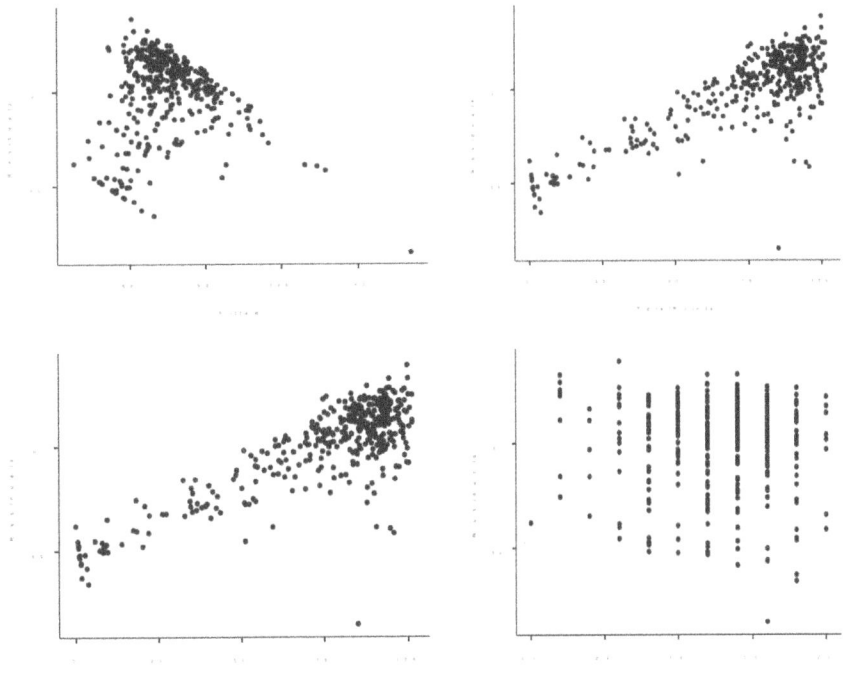

Figure 7.19 *Residual plots of regression analysis.*

The Residual plots show that our data is clumped (Figure 7.19). The plots should have no pattern and be evenly distributed about the 0 on the y axis. Our data is also not evenly distributed in this manner. Though the regression analysis gave us a result, the tests of our data generally indicate that it violates the assumptions of regression and the results we received are not valid. Therefore, there is nothing to report, not even a failed significance test and an unacceptable alternative hypothesis. We need to find a better test for our data.

Here is how the results of the test could be reported if we found no problems with our data:

A multiple linear regression shows that SessionTime, AssessmentTime, and PreTest are significant predictors of TotalPoints ($F(3,393) = 60.9, p < .001$) with an adjusted R^2 of .312.

Additionally, the regression equation can be reported. The multiple linear regression equations is similar to the simple linear regression equation, but with additional terms for each independent variable in the analysis:

The fitted regression model is: TotalPoints = 53.3 + (.000749 * SessionTime) + (.000129 * AssessmentTime) + (12.2 * PreTest).

One-Way ANOVA

ANOVA stands for analysis of variance and is a very useful statistical test that comes in multiple forms. It compares the proportion of variance attributed to the independent variables to the unexplained variance. It works with three or more groups or variables. It is a much better choice than running multiple *t*-tests to cover all the groups or conditions. Multiple *t*-tests inflate the Type I error rate that impacts our ability to draw accurate conclusions (Cronk 2004). The ANOVA test tells us if there is a significant difference between groups, but it does not tell us between which groups. Post hoc tests need to be used to discover that. The one-way ANOVA is the simplest form. It is also called the independent factor ANOVA.

The one-way ANOVA requires that the one dependent variable be continuous and should be "approximately" normally distributed (Goss-Sampson 2019, 85). The one independent variable, or grouping variable, should be categorical. Groups should be independent of each other, and there should be homogeneity of variance between the groups. Outliers may be problematic. If homogeneity, normal distribution, and large outliers are a problem, then the nonparametric version of the one-way ANOVA, known as the Kruskal–Wallis test, should be used.

The one-way ANOVA in jamovi does not have an effect size option, and it has limited options (Wanzer n.d.). Instead from the "ANOVA" menu, select "ANOVA." Using only one independent variable will give the same results as the one-way ANOVA test. Move the dependent variable to the "Dependent Variable" box and the independent variable to the "Fixed Factors" box as seen in Figure 7.20. If this were an ANOVA analysis, we would add additional independent variables to the fixed factor box.

From the 'Effect Size menu," eta^2 (η^2) was selected. Eta^2 has the same value as partial eta^2 in a one-way ANOVA. Partial eta^2 is a better choice when there is more than one fixed factor. It is a biased measure with small sample sizes, but as sample sizes increase, the bias decreases making it a good choice for larger sample sizes (Grace-Martin 2011). Omega^2 (ω^2) is an unbiased measure that should be used when sample sizes are small ("Effect Sizes for ANOVAs" n.d.). The value of omega^2 will be smaller than eta^2. These values are read like an R^2. They account for a percentage of the variance. The example output in Figure 7.21 shows an η^2 of .191. We could say that 19 percent of the variance can be explained by this model. Effects sizes are .01 for small effects, .06 for medium effects, and .14 and up for large effect sizes for either η^2 or ω^2. We have a large effect size.

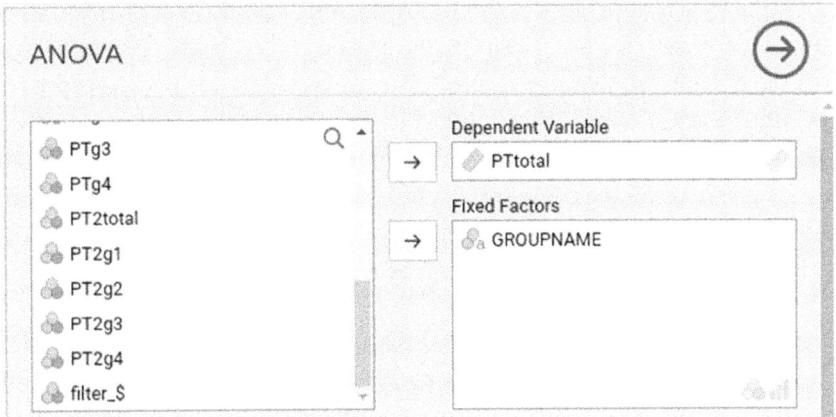

Figure 7.20 *Selecting variables for ANOVA analysis.*

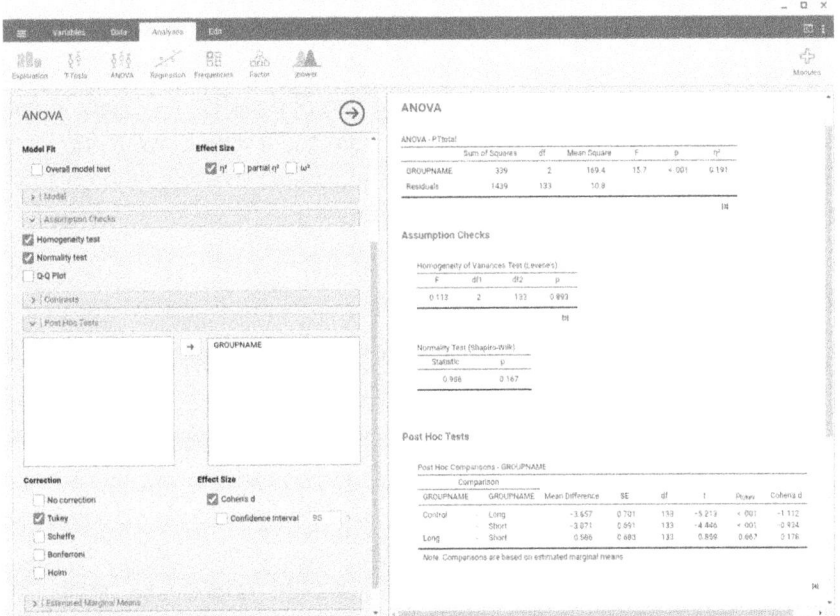

Figure 7.21 *One-way ANOVA results with selected tests.*

On the "Assumption Checks" menu, the homogeneity and normality tests were selected to see if our data meets the required assumptions. Both tests have nonsignificant *p*-values indicating that the data does meet the necessary requirements. A Q-Q plot would show the linear relationship of the data, but was not selected.

On the "Post Hoc Tests" menu, under "Correction," "Tukey" was selected. Tukey's is a standard post hoc test. "Holm" is also a good choice. Under "Effect Size" on that same menu, "Cohen's d" was selected to see the effect size between specific groups. The result of the Tukey's tests, listed as Ptukey because it is a p-value, shows significant differences between the long group and the control group, and the short group and the control group, but no difference between the long and short groups. Cohen's d for the two significant effects is very large.

Here is how the results of the test can be reported:

A one-way ANOVA showed a significant difference between groups on post-test scores ($F(2, 133) = 15.5$, $p < .001$, $\eta^2 = .191$). A post hoc comparison using Tukey determined that in the long group ($M = 11.4$, $SD = 3.33$) outperformed the control group ($M = 7.72$, $SD = 3.13$, $p < .001$, $d = 1.112$), and the short group ($M = 10.8$, $SD = 3.38$) also performed better than the control group ($M = 7.72$, $SD = 3.13$, $p < .001$, $d = .934$). There was no significant difference between the long and the short groups ($p = .667$).

The mean and standard deviation are not part of the ANOVA analysis. To get them, descriptive statistics had to be run from the "Explorations" menu with "PTtotal" placed in the "Variables" box, and "Groupname" moved to the "Split by" box to get the values needed for reporting purposes.

ANOVA

An ANOVA has two or more independent variables in the "Fixed Factors" box, compared to the one-way ANOVA that has only one. This type of ANOVA is also called a factorial ANOVA. A 3 × 2 factorial ANOVA has two independent variables. The first variable has three levels as in our previous example of control, long, and short. The other factor would have two levels. In our case, we will add an ID number for two high schools.

We will be brief in discussing the ANOVA. We added one additional independent variable to the analysis. We added a high school ID number. This is what makes our analysis a 3 × 2 factorial ANOVA. Then we changed the "Effect Size" to partial η^2. Under the "Post Hoc Test" menu, there are now three choices: "Groupname," "HS#," and "Groupname * HS#." The latter represents the interaction between these two groups. All three of these choices were moved to the box on the right-hand side.

The results of the ANOVA are seen in Figure 7.22. Looking at the p-values and the partial η^2, we see a strong relationship between PTtotal and Groupname.

ANOVA

ANOVA - PTtotal

	Sum of Squares	df	Mean Square	F	p	η²p
GROUPNAME	357.1	2	178.5	17.10	<.001	0.208
HS#	42.8	1	42.8	4.10	0.045	0.031
GROUPNAME ✻ HS#	43.0	2	21.5	2.06	0.132	0.031
Residuals	1356.9	130	10.4			

[3]

Figure 7.22 *Factorial ANOVA results.*

Post Hoc Tests

Post Hoc Comparisons - GROUPNAME ✻ HS#

GROUPNAME	HS#		GROUPNAME	HS#	Mean Difference	SE	df	t	P tukey	Cohen's d
Control	1	-	Control	2	-1.845	1.019	130	-1.810	0.463	-0.571
		-	Long	1	-3.688	1.084	130	-3.403	0.011	-1.141
		-	Long	2	-5.718	1.034	130	-5.528	<.001	-1.770
		-	Short	1	-4.487	1.084	130	-4.141	<.001	-1.389
		-	Short	2	-4.045	1.012	130	-3.995	0.001	-1.252
	2	-	Long	1	-1.843	0.953	130	-1.933	0.387	0.570
		-	Long	2	-3.873	0.897	130	-4.319	<.001	-1.199
		-	Short	1	-2.643	0.953	130	-2.773	0.068	0.818
		-	Short	2	-2.200	0.871	130	-2.524	0.125	-0.681
Long	1	-	Long	2	-2.030	0.969	130	-2.094	0.297	-0.628
		-	Short	1	-0.800	1.022	130	-0.783	0.970	-0.248
		-	Short	2	-0.357	0.946	130	-0.378	0.999	-0.111
	2	-	Short	1	1.230	0.969	130	1.269	0.801	-0.381
		-	Short	2	1.673	0.889	130	1.882	0.418	0.518
Short	1	-	Short	2	0.443	0.946	130	0.468	0.997	0.137

Note. Comparisons are based on estimated marginal means

Post Hoc Comparisons - HS#

HS#		HS#	Mean Difference	SE	df	t	P tukey	Cohen's d
1	-	2	-1.14	0.565	130	-2.02	0.045	-0.354

Note. Comparisons are based on estimated marginal means

Figure 7.23 *Post hoc test for factorial ANOVA.*

When examining the effect of one of the named factors, it is called a main effect. There is also a small effect between HS# and PTtotal but no significant interaction between PTtotal and Groupname.

The same assumption checks and the Q-Q plot were used to make sure the data worked with a parametric test, which it does. Tukey's post hoc test was used along with Cohen's *d*. The next big portion of the output is the post hoc tests, because "Groupname * HS#" lists every interaction. The image in Figure 7.23 also shows the difference between high schools 1 and 2. Further down the page is the post hoc comparison between the groups in Groupname. This is identical to the information seen in Figure 7.21, so it is not repeated here.

The results present a good deal of information. The individual post hoc comparisons for each of the factors show the aggregated data for those factors and corresponds to the ANOVA results at the top of the results page. We want to see a difference in our Groupname factor because that is where the control and experimental groups are, and we did. Both experimental groups outperformed the control group. We would have preferred to see no significant difference in our HS# factor, which would indicate that students at both schools were performing equally well. However, the post hoc test on HS# shows that high school 2 is outperforming high school 1.

When we look at the post hoc test for "Groupname*HS#," we get more detailed information and see that all the experimental groups outperform the control group from high school 1 with significant p-values and effect sizes. The story is different when examining the control group from high school 2. Only one of the experimental groups outperforms the control in a meaningful way.

Here is how the results of the test can be reported. We could dig more into specific or include the large post hoc table for Groupname*HS# with some additional comments:

> A 3 × 2 factorial ANOVA was used to compare the posttest scores between two experimental and a control group at two different high schools. A significant difference was found for both Groupname ($F(2, 130) = 17.1$, $p < .001$, $\eta^2_p = .208$), and HS# ($F(1, 130) = 4.1$, $p = .045$, $\eta^2_p = .031$). There was no significant interaction between Groupname and HS# ($F(2, 130) = 2.06$, $p = .1321$, $\eta^2_p = .031$).
>
> A post hoc comparison using Tukey determined that in the long group ($M = 11.4$, $SD = 3.33$) outperformed the control group ($M = 7.72$, $SD = 3.13$, $p < .001$, $d = 1.112$), and the short group ($M = 10.8$, $SD = 3.38$) also performed better than the control group ($M = 7.72$, $SD = 3.13$, $p < .001$, $d = .934$). There was no significant difference between the long and the short groups ($p = .667$). The post hoc comparison also showed that high school 2 ($M = 10.4$, $SD = 3.34$) scored better than high school 1 ($M = 9.48$, $SD = 3.97$, $p = .045$, $d = .354$).

There are other variations on the ANOVA that are beyond the scope of this book. For example, repeated measures ANOVA can look at the dependent variable, such as multiple testing, over time and its impact on group members. A mixed factorial ANOVA, for example, adds between-subject factors to the time element in a repeated measures test, allowing you to look at control and treatment groups. An ANCOVA allows you to remove the effect of a known covariate from the analysis. The ANOVA family allows for many types of analysis that are useful to library research.

Summary and Reflection

In this chapter, we looked at the importance of open-source software to statistical analysis. Are you more likely to use jamovi or a commercial package like SPSS for your statistical work? What are your reasons for choosing one over the other? What software would you recommend to your patrons or students?

We looked at a number of statistical tests, the types of information they use, and the results that they give. This was a brief introduction to statistical tests and testing. Without a basic understanding of statistical methods, a lot of the information in research articles is beyond our comprehension. Do you think this information will help you to evaluate the quality of research articles?

Statistical tests can be confusing to do and the output can be difficult to understand. Jamovi makes it easy to run statistical tests. Did this information inspire you to conduct the kinds of research that require the use of inferential statistics? Do you understand how to read the output and what to look for? Does this process now seem easier than you thought?

Implementation

If you have a set of data you can use or, using the sample data supplied with jamovi and JASP, start practicing using jamovi. Begin with an easy test like the one sample *t*-test. Get used to selecting the dependent and independent variables. Choose among the test options, and with each choice, examine the output. Read the output with an eye for reporting your findings whether they are significant or not. Try the test again selecting different variables, if there are others that will work, and examine the results. Try each of the tests you think that you might need to run with the data your research idea would generate. Practice how to use the program and how to read the results.

Vocabulary

ANOVA
Chi-square goodness of fit test

Chi-square test of association
Collinearity
Correlation
Degrees of freedom
Effect size
Homogeneity
Independent samples *t*-test
jamovi
JASP
Linearity
Multiple linear regression
Nonparametric tests
Normality test
One sample *t*-test
One-way ANOVA
Open-source software
Parametric tests
Post hoc tests
Q-Q plot
R
Simple linear regression
Statistical software

References

"Adjusted R2 / Adjusted R-Squared: What Is It Used For?" 2023. Statistics How To. https://www.statisticshowto.com/probability-and-statistics/statistics-definitions/adjusted-r2/.

American Psychological Association. 2019. *Publication Manual of the American Psychological Association*. Seventh edition. Washington, DC: American Psychological Association.

Berg, Ruben Geert van der. 2023. "SPSS Shapiro-Wilk Test." SPSS Tutorials. https://www.spss-tutorials.com/spss-shapiro-wilk-test-for-normality/.

"Chrome OS Quick Setup." n.d. Flatpak. https://flatpak.org/setup/Chrome%20OS. Accessed February 24, 2023.

Connaway, Lynn Silipigni, and Ronald R. Powell. 2010. *Basic Research Methods for Librarians*. Fifth edition. Santa Barbara, CA: Libraries Unlimited.

Connaway, Lynn Silipigni, and Marie L. Radford. 2017. *Research Methods in Library and Information Science*. Sixth edition. Santa Barbara, CA: Libraries Unlimited.

"CRAN - Contributed Packages." n.d. https://cran.r-project.org/web/packages/index.html. Accessed August 30, 2022.

Cronk, Brian C. 2004. *How to Use SPSS: A Step-by-Step Guide to Analysis and Interpretation*. Third edition. Glendale, CA: Pyrczak.

Donnelly, Robert A. 2007. *The Complete Idiot's Guide to Statistics*. 2nd ed. New York: Alpha.

Draws, Tim. 2018. "Teaching with JASP." JASP - Free and User-Friendly Statistical Software. https://jasp-stats.org/teaching-with-jasp/.

"Effect Sizes for ANOVAs." n.d. https://cran.r-project.org/web/packages/effectsize/vignettes/anovaES.html. Accessed March 7, 2023.

Fisher, Tim. 2022. "What Is Freeware?" *Lifewire*. July 7, 2022. https://www.lifewire.com/freeware-definition-4154271.

Frost, Jim. 2017. "How to Interpret the F-Test of Overall Significance in Regression Analysis." *Statistics By Jim* (blog). April 4, 2017. http://statisticsbyjim.com/regression/interpret-f-test-overall-significance-regression/.

Goss-Sampson, Mark. 2019. "Statistical Analysis in JASP – A Students Guide v0.10.2." *figshare*. https://doi.org/10.6084/M9.FIGSHARE.9980744.

Grace-Martin, Karen. 2011. "A Comparison of Effect Size Statistics." *The Analysis Factor* (blog). January 13, 2011. https://www.theanalysisfactor.com/effect-size/.

"Hamburger Button." 2023. In Wikipedia. https://en.wikipedia.org/w/index.php?title=Hamburger_button&oldid=1138440398.

"Jamovi." n.d. UConn Software Catalog. https://software.uconn.edu/software/jamovi/. Accessed September 6, 2022.

"Jamovi." n.d. Flathub. https://flathub.org/apps/details/org.jamovi.jamovi. Accessed February 24, 2023

"Jamovi Statistical Software." 2022. https://www.isu.edu/ichr/resources/jamovi-statistical-software/.

"Jamovi: Stats. Open. Now." n.d. https://www.jamovi.org/. Accessed April 11, 2022.

The jamovi project (n.d.). Jamovi (Version 2.3) [Computer Software]. https://www.jamovi.org.

Kermer, Debby. 2022. "Software for Digital Scholarship: Jamovi." George Mason University: InfoGuides. September 1. https://infoguides.gmu.edu/software/jamovi.

"List of Universities Using Jamovi to Teach Stats." n.d. Jamovi. https://forum.jamovi.org/viewtopic.php?f=2&t=2105. Accessed September 6, 2022.

Midrack, Renee Lynn. 2021. "What Is Open Source Software?" *Lifewire*. March 7. https://www.lifewire.com/what-is-open-source-software-4147547.

Muenchen, Bob. 2019. "A Comparative Review of the JASP Statistical Software." *R-Bloggers* (blog). April 18, 2019. https://www.r-bloggers.com/2019/04/a-comparative-review-of-the-jasp-statistical-software/.

Navarro, Danielle J., and David R. Foxcroft. 2018. *Learning Statistics with Jamovi: A Tutorial for Psychology Students and Other Beginners*. https://doi.org/10.24384/HGC3-7P15.

"PSPP – GNU Project - Free Software Foundation." 2020. ttps://www.gnu.org/software/pspp/.

"R (Programming Language)." 2022. In *Wikipedia*. https://en.wikipedia.org/w/index.php?title=R_(programming_language)&oldid=1106593055.

"SAS (Software)." 2022. In *Wikipedia*. https://en.wikipedia.org/w/index.php?title=SAS_(software)&oldid=1100293679.

"SPSS." 2022. In *Wikipedia*. https://en.wikipedia.org/w/index.php?title=SPSS&oldid=1095491591.

Stephanie. 2022. "Shapiro-Wilk Test: Definition, How to Run It in SPSS." *Statistics How To*. March 28. https://www.statisticshowto.com/shapiro-wilk-test/.

"User Guide." n.d. Jamovi. https://www.jamovi.org/user-manual.html. Accessed May 12, 2022.

Wanzer, Dana. n.d. "Statistics with Jamovi." https://danawanzer.github.io/stats-with-jamovi/. Accessed November 4, 2022.

Zach. 2019. "A Guide to Multicollinearity & VIF in Regression." *Statology* (blog). March 10. https://www.statology.org/multicollinearity-regression/.

8 Sharing Your Research with Others

> ### Essential Questions
>
> Use these questions to guide your reading:
> - How can we best translate our research results to stakeholders and decision-makers?
> - What are some potential outlets for sharing the results of your research?
> - How does disseminating our research benefit the field of librarianship?
> - What are some nontraditional methods for sharing our research with others?

Introduction

The previous chapter discussed running and interpreting statistical tests including correlations, regressions, t-tests, ANOVA, and chi-square tests in the freeware program jamovi. It also covered how to read and interpret the results and how to prepare them for sharing. In Chapter 1, we introduced the idea of conducting original research to advocate for your library or compete for funding within your own institution, but the applicability of a research success story is valued beyond the walls of your organization as well. If your original intention was to conduct research to answer a workplace problem, this chapter will provide guidance to help you translate the message to decision-makers at your institution. This chapter will also help with formalizing your results to share beyond your workplace and help contribute to the larger conversations in the field.

Evaluation and Transfer

As librarians, we are aware of the importance of evaluating information for reliability, relevance, authority, bias, currency, and accuracy, but it bears repeating here. No original research process is complete without a good deal of evaluation: both of the information resources selected, methods conducted, data collected, and end product developed. Reflection is a key piece of the research process as it not only helps us to improve our process and product but also aids in the transfer of new knowledge to other contexts (Griggs et al. 2018; Schön 1983, 1987). By taking an analytical approach to reviewing our own work, we are more likely to improve the process next time and apply the lessons learned to our practice. Different outputs require different levels of evaluation; the process may be extensive and iterative for a grant project so that we ensure the satisfaction of the funding agency's requirements and briefer for a board meeting presentation, but evaluation should always be a key piece of our process throughout our research endeavors.

Sharing Your Message with Stakeholders

Whatever the original motivation for conducting original research—be it continuing education, promotion and tenure requirements, or simply a problem to be solved—you may be considering the value of sharing those results with the administrative decision-makers at your institution. Depending on the size of your library, these leaders may be outside of the library and therefore require careful consideration in how you present your message. When advocating for your library to stakeholders outside of the field of librarianship, it's important to first understand what those administrators value, so that you can craft your message in line with their priorities (Kachel 2016, 54). An institutional mission, vision, or strategic plan can be a good place to start understanding where your research problem fits into the bigger picture. Spend some time reflecting or discussing your ideas with colleagues for feedback; perhaps they have some insight based on previous experience communicating with leadership that can benefit your approach. Don't feel discouraged if, at first, the institutional values do not obviously align with what your library needs. Often, with some information about what pressing issues are at the forefront of an administrator's priorities, you can craft your message in a way that speaks to helping both of your causes; rather than simply making a request for resources, you can pitch your ask in a way that will also address their concerns, making it more likely to be heard (Dando 2014; Levitov 2012, 88–9).

Consider this example: A school librarian forges a successful collaboration with her local therapy animal association to encourage reluctant readers and foster a love of reading in her school community. She wants to ask her principal for funding to expand the program but the district at-large is prioritizing improving standardized test scores and funding is highly competitive. She knows that for her request to be successful, she will need to position it to address the administration's highest priority. Though her initial motivation was to encourage leisure reading, her hypothesis is that the more students read for pleasure, the better their reading comprehension will be and higher standardized reading scores should follow. She designs a study with these goals in mind. The proposal for her school library programming can be a win-win, as long as she pitches it to align with the goals of her broader learning community.

Another important consideration is getting to know what type of information your stakeholders value: Are they motivated by data and statistics, or anecdotes and stories? (Kachel 2017) Answering this question can help you decide whether to take a qualitative or quantitative approach to sharing your research. In the example above, the librarian knows that her data-driven administration team will want to see evidence and plans to conduct research over the course of the fall term so she can make her request in the spring. The medium is also an important factor that can impact how your message is received. A written report, slide presentation, or infographic all present data in different ways: which is the most fitting for your information, setting, and audience? How much time will you be given to communicate these findings? Will it happen in-person or electronically? Do you need to prepare a brief elevator pitch or an eye-catching annual report? Answering these questions will help you decide how to move forward with sharing your message.

Most fields are filled with specialized jargon that is difficult for nonexperts to understand, and the library world is no different. If you are communicating your findings to stakeholders outside of the field—or even your specific subfield—it will be important to clarify or avoid using specialized jargon. Even within librarianship subfields such as cataloging, archiving, and instructing are unique terminology, acronyms, and vocabulary that should be clarified carefully when crafting this communication across departments (YALSA 2017). Last, it is crucial to "close the loop" and by communicating the results, the impact on users, and demonstrating the responsible use of resources to shore up future support (Beckett 2016).

Contributing to the Field

There are many potential avenues for sharing your research with others. Beyond the stakeholders at your institution, there are entire professional organizations dedicated to answering similar questions and sharing the results. Some of your options include presenting at a conference, publishing your work in a scholarly journal, or contributing to a trade publication. For each of these avenues, the spectrum of formality, audience, reach, and impact varies greatly. A conference presentation is typically delivered while the research is in earlier stages and allows opportunities for gathering and implementing feedback from the field, whereas a journal publication often represents a more complete report of the research. A conference proceedings paper can often be expanded into a scholarly journal article as the research progresses (González-Albo and Bordons 2011).

Publication

There are many avenues to consider when pondering the publication of your research. Contributing to a trade publication in your field can be viewed as a lower-stakes option since there is not an extensive process of double-blind peer-review to go through. However, we should be careful not to conflate low stakes with low impact. Many professionals subscribe to trade publications through their professional organizations and read these articles as part of their ongoing professional development. Often written for a more general, rather than specialized, audience can mean that the potential reach of trade publications is greater. Contributing a publication on your research to one of these sources is an impactful way to share the lessons you learned in the study you conducted. These publications are typically edited rather than peer-reviewed. Most trade publications will share submission information, themed issues, instructions, and deadlines on their websites.

The more formal option is submitting your article for peer-review in a scholarly journal. There are likely many to choose from depending on the subtopic of your research. The peer-review process is longer and may include iterations of revisions, resubmissions, or even rejections. Within the peer-reviewed realm, you may also choose an open-access educational journal, which typically entails a cost incurred by the author, but grants free access for readers. The open-access movement in library and information science is growing and provides greater visibility for our hard-earned research endeavors (Barik and Jena 2019; Li, Liu, and Wang 2021; Mukherjee 2009). The general format for publishing original research results is the acronym IMRAD, which stands for introduction, methodology, results, and discussion (Cooper 2015).

Presentation

Another route for sharing your research is to present at a local, regional, national, or even international conference. These can range from short lightning talks to hour-long panels or presentations. The publication component here often takes the shape of a conference proceedings paper that goes through an editorial process as well. Again, while a national or international conference may sound more prestigious and certainly have a broader reach, it can be just as impactful to your local community to present at a state or regional conference.

When choosing the outlet for sharing your research, it is tempting to speak to those who would most appreciate the topic at hand—others in your field. However, a conference of like-minded peers may not always be the ones to impact decisions and make change. Consider breaking down this silo by presenting in an adjacent field. Research demonstrates that decision-makers often operate in their own echo chambers, influenced by research within their curated bubble alone. By bringing your research to their preferred outlets and venues, you can help diversify and shape decision-making (Goldie et al. 2014, 296). This will depend on the goals and outcomes of your particular research, for instance, research about school libraries shared at a conference for school principals rather than an audience of other school librarians.

Similar to the scale of publications, the variety of options for conference presentations also comes with a range of preparation and rigor in the submission process. A local conference may only require a brief abstract and a submission deadline of a few months prior, whereas a national conference proposal may require much more detail and need to be submitted over a year in advance. Surveying the field for the outlets that would be most interested in hearing about your work can help you plan accordingly.

Nontraditional Methods

Outside of the traditional publication or presentation options, there are many emerging and nontraditional ways to share your research outcomes. Social media is a blossoming area for scholars to informally share their work. Posts, live streaming, blogs, and TED Talks are some of the informal social media outlets for sharing scholarly information. In some fields, social media is seen as an important way to communicate scholarly literature to a broader, more general audience of nonexperts to combat the proliferation of misinformation on social networking channels (Bentz et al. 2021). Deemed "social scholarship," emerging frameworks expand on previous concepts of scholarship and support incorporating this type of work into our professional practices (Greenhow et al. 2019). Bringing scholarly communication to social media also increases access to those without the information privilege of subscription access to peer-reviewed journals or the funds to travel to conferences in global destinations.

Of course, any of these options for sharing your research can be combined. A presentation can be expanded to turn into a publication and the resulting discussion can be shared widely in social media circles. Find your like-minded researchers in these publication and professional organization circles and there will be no shortage of opportunities to expand and share your future undertakings. Your research may immediately benefit your institution, but publishing or presenting to share your results with broader audiences can positively impact the field outside of your local sphere of influence. You can also benefit from creating a professional learning network, making new contacts, and looking forward to getting together with your collaborators for future research endeavors.

Mentorship and Collaboration

For those who may feel daunted by the added time that sharing your research can entail, consider collaboration or mentorship with a colleague to lighten the workload. While newer hires may benefit from the mentorship of their senior colleagues, they may also bring fresh ideas, perspectives, and skills to the collaboration, making these partnerships mutually beneficial. Rarely are research projects solo endeavors in our field. It just takes reading a few scholarly articles or attending a conference to sense the obvious benefits, collegiality, and positive impact of a trusted coauthor. As the scholarly landscape becomes more familiar, inviting graduate or undergraduate students to join your project can be a great benefit to the field by mentoring the next generation of scholars (Ferris 2019).

Collaboration between institutions is another effective approach to combine limited resources, which reduces silos and the duplication of efforts (Jaeger et al. 2017). Consider reaching out beyond peer institutions to forge research partnerships between school, academic, public libraries, and beyond. These partnerships can expand research efforts and distribute the increased workload. This important work goes beyond providing essential services and helps all parties reap the rewards of demonstrating library value (Wynia 2022). Research partnerships may be a particularly important approach when considering the subfields of public and school librarianship, as the requirements for publication for these practitioners tend to lack, but the need for representation within the research does not (Adkins 2019; Latham and Lenstra 2020).

Summary and Reflection

The immediate applicability of our research endeavors is likely within the walls of our own institutions—if we can get the decision-makers on board. What new strategies will you try in crafting your message to stakeholders? Beyond the walls of our respective institutions, sharing our research benefits the field at-large by offering solutions to questions that others may also be struggling with. Research dissemination drives our field forward, fosters innovation, and can result in meaningful networking and collaboration. What professional events can you attend in order to forge new research partnerships? There are countless methods—both formal and informal—to disseminate the results of your original research project. From presentation to publication and social media posts to TED Talks, the sky is the limit. What modes of sharing inspire you to get involved?

Implementation

Reflect on which mode of sharing your research will best meet your personal and professional goals. If you prefer publication, look up the most relevant periodicals related to your topic and review their submission guidelines, including deadlines. If you prefer to present, check out the upcoming conferences related to your research interest, find the next conference date, and review the call for proposals. If your end product has already been determined—a dissertation or internal report, for instance—how can you extend your research to the broader library community?

Vocabulary

Echo chamber

References

Adkins, Denice. 2019. "Journals, Subjects, and Authors of Research Literature on Public Libraries: An Analysis." *Public Library Quarterly* 38, no. 2: 211–33.

Barik, Nilaranjan, and Puspanjali Jena. 2019. "Bibliometric Portrait of Select Open Access Journals in the Field of Library and Information Science: A Scopus Based Analysis." *Library Philosophy and Practice*: 1–18.

Beckett, Edith K. 2016. "Influences on New Jersey Public Library Budget Requests." *Bottom Line* 29, no. 2: 86–96.

Bentz, Nathaniel, Emily Chase, and Paige DeLoach. 2021. "Social Media Debate Position 4: Social Media and Information Services." *Internet Reference Services Quarterly* 25, nos. 1–2: 55–64.

Cooper, I. Diane. 2015. "How to Write an Original Research Paper (and Get It Published)." *Journal of the Medical Library Association: JMLA* 103, no. 2: 67.

Dando, Priscille. 2014. *Say It with Data: A Concise Guide to Making Your Case and Getting Results*. Chicago: American Library Association.

Ferris, Dana R. 2019. "Guiding Junior Scholars into and through the Publication Process." In *Novice Writers and Scholarly Publication: Authors, Mentors, Gatekeepers*, edited by Pejman Habibie and Ken Hyland, London: Palgrave Macmillan, 215–31.

Goldie, David, Matthew Linick, Huriya Jabbar, and Christopher Lubienski. 2014. "Using Bibliometric and Social Media Analyses to Explore the "Echo Chamber" Hypothesis." *Educational Policy* 28, no. 2: 281–305.

González-Albo, Borja, and María Bordons. 2011. "Articles vs. Proceedings Papers: Do They Differ in Research Relevance and Impact? A Case Study in the Library and Information Science Field." *Journal of Infometrics* 5, no. 3: 369–81. DOI: 10.1016/j.joi.2011.01.011

Greenhow, Christine, Benjamin Gleason, and K. Bret Staudt Willet. 2019. "Social Scholarship Revisited: Changing Scholarly Practices in the Age of Social Media." *British Journal of Educational Technology* 50, no. 3: 987–1004.

Griggs, Vivienne, Richard Holden, Aileen Lawless, and Jan Rae. 2018. "From Reflective Learning to Reflective Practice: Assessing Transfer." *Studies in Higher Education* 43, no. 7: 1172–83.

Jaeger, Paul T., Erin Zerhusen, Ursula Gorham, Renee F. Hill, and Natalie Greene Taylor. 2017. "Waking Up to Advocacy in a New Political Reality for Libraries." *Library Quarterly* 87, no. 4: 350–68.

Kachel, Debra. 2016. "Growing Your Roots of Influence." *Teacher Librarian* 43, no. 4: 53.

Kachel, Debra. 2017. "The Advocacy Continuum." *Teacher Librarian* 44, no. 3: 50.

Latham, Joyce M., and Noah Lenstra. 2021. "Researching Practice/Practicing Research: The Public Library in Partnership with Academia." *Library Trends* 69, no. 4: 717–24.

Levitov, Deborah D. 2012. *Activism and the School Librarian: Tools for Advocacy and Survival*. Santa Barbara, CA: ABC-CLIO.

Li, Huixu, Lanjian Liu, and Xianwen Wang. 2021. "The Open Access Effect in Social Media Exposure of Scholarly Articles: A Matched-Pair Analysis." *Journal of Infometrics* 15, no. 3: 101154.

Mukherjee, Bhaskar. 2009. "Do Open-Access Journals in Library and Information Science Have Any Scholarly Impact? A Bibliometric Study of Selected Open-Access Journals Using Google Scholar." *Journal of the American Society for Information Science and Technology* 60, no. 3: 581–94.

Schön, Donald A. 1983. *The Reflective Practitioner*. New York: Basic Books.

Schön, Donald A. 1987. *Educating the Reflective Practitioner: Toward a New Design for Teaching and Learning in the Professions*. Hoboken, NJ: Jossey-Bass.

Wynia Baluk, Kaitlin, Nicole K. Dalmer, Leora Sas van der Linden, Lisa Radha Weaver, and James Gillett. 2022. "Towards a Research Platform: Partnering for Sustainable and Impactful Research in Public Libraries." *Public Library Quarterly* 42, no. 1: 71–91.

Young Adult Library Services Association (YALSA). 2017. "YALSA Advocacy Toolkit 2017."

9 Putting It All Together

> **Essential Questions**
>
> Use these questions to guide your reading:
> - Of the topics covered in this book, what were the most useful for your intended purpose?
> - What topics might you need to revisit?

Introduction

The previous chapter discussed the various ways you can share your research with others via traditional and nontraditional methods. This is an important step in the research process and for our profession. In this chapter, we will review and summarize what was shared throughout this text.

Conducting Original Research for Your Library

Conducting original research is a major undertaking for librarians at every level, but there is great potential to reap rewards when it is executed correctly and shared effectively. Each librarian will have their own motivations for conducting research—be it a job requirement, continuing education, data-driven decision-making, or the satisfaction of contributing to moving the field forward. By engaging in the process of conducting original research, we can become better practitioners, better colleagues, better teachers, and better leaders. Entering the scholarly conversation empowers us and is valued in our profession at all levels and specialties. Conducting original research can also inspire change, convince decision-makers, provide answers, and connect us to the communities we serve in meaningful ways.

A good research project should have a scope that is appropriate to the task—and resources—at hand. Selecting a topic on which to conduct original research is intertwined with exploring the existing body of scholarly literature to determine which questions have already been answered and where gaps in the body of knowledge exist. Inspiration can be drawn from the "Searching to Learn" process to broaden or narrow your approach. Utilizing all of the tools in your library toolbox such as databases, Boolean searching, and interlibrary loan will assure you've accessed all of the information needed to conduct a thorough review of the literature.

Writing a formal literature review may be optional depending on the type of research you undertake and how you plan to disseminate the results, but even where it is not required, surveying the literature is still a good practice. Doing so will introduce you to the current scholarly conversations happening around your topic, help you to build upon others' ideas rather than replicate their efforts, and even inspire new avenues for your own research. There are free tools you can use to organize and synthesize your writing. Familiarizing yourself with a reference manager such as EndNote, Mendeley, or Zotero will help you collect, organize, and cite your sources. A synthesis matrix is also recommended to help facilitate writing that synthesizes rather than simply summarizes and helps to highlight your unique thoughts on the topic.

When you have a problem or a question that needs to be addressed, consider the nature of the problem. Does this question require research to be answered? If the answer is yes, then consider the types of data you need to collect and who you need to get that information from. Formulate a hypothesis to guide you through the research process. Your hypothesis should help you determine whether you are doing qualitative or quantitative research or taking a mixed-method approach. With a broad understanding of what you want to answer via your hypothesis and how you will approach your research question, dive into research methods and find a method that is appropriate for your question and the data you plan to collect. With a hypothesis and research method in hand, you are ready to begin collecting data.

Data may already exist that will answer or partially answer your research question. You need to identify sources of data that may help you. The data can come from within your library through your various systems, or from school districts, state, and federal agencies. If these sources do not address your research question, then you will need to collect data. You will have to decide who you need information from, how you are going to collect it, and develop the tools you need to gather the information you want. You will need to develop a data management plan that addresses how you will collect, de-identify, store, and ultimately dispose of the data. You should also include a plan for sharing your data for the benefit of future research. Finally, after all your data is collected, you should look at descriptive statistics it generates. This will help you get a feel for the data and begin to see the story it has to tell.

Understanding descriptive statistics is a good starting point, but you need to learn more about statistics to become statistically literate and to better understand the statistical tests you will be using with your data. It is important to know that a Type I error is a false positive and a Type II error is a false negative, and how these errors can be mitigated. Statistical significance is a vitally important concept in statistical testing and tells you whether you can accept or need to reject your hypothesis. Practical significance needs to be considered to ensure that there are real-world effects being found. Calculating effect sizes and knowing how to interpret them for each statistical test helps you to understand what the results of the test are saying. Having enough subjects participating in your study reduces the chances of Type I and Type II errors, improves the odds for finding significant results, and may even allow you to generalize the results of your research to other similar populations beyond your institution while adding to the knowledge base of library science.

Statistical software has come a long way since the days of mainframe computers. Open-source software like jamovi is free to use, has an intuitive graphical user interface, and runs on multiple platforms supporting a democratization of statistical analysis. It includes t-tests which you can use to compare mean scores between groups or within a group to see if your instruction improved outcomes. Chi-square tests are important because they allow you to compare categorical data and see if any of that data is underperforming or outperforming what you expected. Correlations and regressions show you how strong the relationship is between things. ANOVAs measure the differences between and within groups and the proportion of the difference that each factor has on the outcome. With jamovi and knowledge of how to run, interpret, and report the results of statistical tests, you will be able to find an answer to the question you posed while helping your library, building your skills and career, and supporting our profession.

Equipped with these tools and best practices, your original research will no doubt be a success worth sharing. Be sure to carefully evaluate any information resources you cite as well as your overall process and product. To effectively translate your research outcomes from library jargon to language your stakeholders can appreciate, take the time to understand the priorities and preferred communication style of these decision-makers. Conference presentations and publications are the traditional means of disseminating research, but other avenues are worth exploring as well. Sharing your research at your local level as well as to the broader professional networks helps to move the field of librarianship forward.

Implementation

Our goal in writing this book is to show that no matter who you are or what type of library you work in, you can use research methods to solve the problems you encounter in your libraries. You can develop a study that will improve your skills as a librarian and increase the knowledge base of the profession. It will take some planning and additional work, but research is not the domain of the few. To be truly effective in advancing our profession, research needs to be practiced and shared at all levels and in all corners of librarianship.

Index

academic libraries, 15
action research, 37, 42
adjusted R2, 113
advanced search techniques, 16
advocacy, 2, 4
AIC, 114
alternative hypothesis, 36, 40, 82
American Association of School
    Librarians, 5, 10
American Community Survey, 58
American Library, 10
ANCOVA, 124
ANOVA, 119, 122, 143
APA Publication Manual, 102
applied research, 36, 37
Association of College and Research
    Libraries, 10
Association of Research Libraries, 66

background information, 12, 14
bar chart, 108
basic research, 34, 36
Bayesian statistical tests, 98
BiblioCommons, 58
bibliometrics, 42
BIC, 114
Blackboard, 65
Boolean operators, 16, 17, 18, 140
box plot, 72
budget, 1, 4, 14

Canvas, 64
case study, 42, 89
catalog, 25
cataloging systems, 58
categorical scale data, 40
causal comparative study, 42
causal research, 4
cause and effect, 38
Center for Open Science, 67
chi-square test of independence. *See*
    test of association
chi-square tests, 105, 129, 142

citation, 27
citation analysis, 42
citation chaining, 27
classroom research, 50
Cohen's *d*, 87, 123
cohort study. *See* longitudinal study
collaboration, 130, 134
collinearity, 113, 116
collinearity statistics, 115, 116
Common Core of Data, 64
conference proceedings, 132
conference proposal, 133
confidence interval, 86
confidence level, 86
content analysis, 42
continuous scale data, 41
control group, 37
convenience sampling, 83
convergent parallel design, 41
Cook's distance, 115, 117
correlation, 42, 87
correlations, 88, 109, 111, 143
COUNTER, 58. *See* COUNTER statistics
COUNTER report, 59
COUNTER statistics, 47
County Business Patterns, 58
Cramer's V, 107
critical thinking, 24
Customer Relationship Management
    System, 56

data, 56, 80, 142
data analysis, 3
Data Ethics Decision Aid, 66
data management plan, 64, 142
data sharing, 66
data storage, 66
data types, 103
database, 12, 15, 140
database report, 59
decennial census, 58
decimal, 99

deductive research, 35
degrees of freedom, 102, 105, 111
Department of Health and Human Services, 34, 49
descriptive statistics, 68, 69, 122, 142
df. *See* degrees of freedom
digital library, 15
dissemination, 135
DMPTool, 66
Durbin–Watson test, 115

echo chamber, 133
Economic Census, 58
effect size, 84, 86, 87, 119, 122, 142
EndNote, 27, 140
eta2. *See* η2
ethical research, 49, 51
ethnography, 42
evaluation, 129
evidence-based librarianship, 5
ex post facto. *See* causal comparative study
Excel, 58, 98
exclude cases analysis by analysis, 101
exclude cases listwise, 101
exempt review, 49
expedited review, 50
experimental design. *See* experimental research
experimental group, 37, 45
experimental research, 37
Exploration tab, 69
external validity, 90

F statistics, 112
F test, 111
facets. *See* limiters
factorial ANOVA, 122
factorial designs, 42
FAIR data principles, 67
false negative, 81, 142
false positive, 81, 142
focus groups, 49
Framework for Information Literacy for Higher Education, 10
full board review, 50

G*Power, 84
Gale Engage, 56
Gamma, 108

gap analysis, 44
generalizability, 88
goodness of fit, 105, 106
Google Analytics, 47, 58
Google Forms, 64
Google Scholar, 16, 25, 27
Google Sheets, 59, 87
grounded theory, 44
grouping variable, 103, 119

histogram, 71, 72
Holm, 122
homogeneity, 103, 113, 119
hypothesis, 3, 35, 131, 140, 142

ID, 122
independent samples *t*-test, 104
inductive research, 35
information, 56, 80
information literacy, 3
informed consent, 50
Innovative Interfaces, 56
Institute of Museum and Library Services, 61
institutional review board, 49
Institutional Review Board, 65
integer, 41, 99
Integrated Postsecondary Education Data System, 61
interlibrary loan, 21, 26, 140
interlibrary loan systems, 58
internal validity, 90
interpretive research, 44
Inter-University Consortium for Political and Social Research, 66
interval scale data, 40
IPEDS. *See* Integrated Postsecondary Education Data System
IRB. *See* Institutional Review Board

jamovi, 68, 69, 71, 84, 85, 88, 96, 97, 98, 142
    effect size, 101
    modules, 84
JASP, 98

Kendall's tau-b, 108
Kruskal–Wallis test, 119

Learning Management System, 64
LibAnswers, 58

LibQual, 44
library engagement platform, 56
library management system, 56
LibreOffice Calc, 59, 98
life history, 44
Likert scale, 47
limiters, 16, 18
literature review, 4, 14, 23, 24, 25, 26, 28, 29, 30, 140
longitudinal study, 45

main effect, 123
Mantel–Haenszel, 108
margin of error, 86
Master Report, 59
maximum, 70
mean, 69, 70
measurement scales, 40
measures of central tendency, 69
median, 40, 69, 70, 72
Mendeley, 27, 140
mentorship, 134
meta-analysis, 45, 67
metadata, 67
minimal risk, 49, 50
minimum, 70
misinformation, 133
missing values, 101
mixed factorial ANOVA, 124
mixed methods research, 41
mode, 71
Model Builder, 114
Moodle, 65
multicollinearity, 116
multiple linear regression, 113

n, 83
N, 83. *See* population
narrative review, 45, 47
National Center for Educational Statistics, 60
National Institutes of Health, 66
National School Library Standards, 10
National Teacher and Principal Survey, 63
negative correlation, 42, 88
nominal scale data, 40
nonexperimental reserach, 38
nonparametric, 105, 107, 109
nonprobability sampling, 84

non-random assignment. *See* quasi-experimental research
nonresponse bias, 90
normal distribution, 68, 71
normality test, 101, 115
null hypothesis, 36, 40
numeric scale data, 100

OCLC, 56
omega2. *See* ω^2
one sample t-test, 102
one-way ANOVA, 119, 122
open- access, 16
Open Educational Resources, 4
open notebook science, 67
open science, 67
Open Science Foundation, 67
open-access, 132
openlabnotebooks.org, 67
open-source software, 39, 97
ordinal scale data, 40
original research, 1, 2, 3, 5, 6, 9, 30, 130, 132, 139, 140
outliers, 72, 119

paired samples t-test, 104
parametric test, 104, 105, 109
partial eta2, 119
Patron Point, 58
paywall, 16, 25
Pearson's correlation coefficient, 88, 108
Pearson's r, 88, 109
peer-review, 132
Phi, 107
phrase operator, 20
PICO, 11, 21
placebo, 37
platform report, 59
population, 38, 83
positive correlation, 42
post hoc tests, 119
posttest, 45, 46, 104
posttest only method, 46
power, 81
power analysis, 84
power level, 84
practical significance, 82, 142
predictor variables, 113

pre-experimental design, 45
pretest, 46, 104
pretest–posttest method, 46
pretest–posttest using intact groups, 45
primary source, 2
principal investigator, 50
privacy, 49, 65, 66
probability sampling, 83
professional development, 132
professional learning network, 134
professional organization, 134
program evaluation, 46
Project COUNTER, 58
PSPP, 97
Ptukey. *See* Tukey's
public libraries, 5, 10, 15
Public Libraries Survey, 61
publication, 132, 135
publication bias, 68
p-value, 82

Q-Q plot, 71, 101, 121
qualitative data, 39, 49, 56
qualitative research, 39, 140
Qualtrics, 64, 87
quantitative data, 56
quantitative research, 39, 40, 140
quartiles, 72
quasi-experimental research, 36
quota sampling, 84

R, 39, 97, 111
R statistic, 111
R2, 113
R2 statistic, 111
random assignment, 38, 46, 90
random sampling, 83
randomized controlled trial, 46
ratio scale data, 41
ratios, 61, 68
reference management program, 27, 28, 30, 140
reflection, 130
registered reports, 68
regression equation, 118
regressions, 143
repeated measures ANOVA, 124
replication studies, 11, 21, 25
reproducibility, 47, 67

research, 35, 36
Research and Assessment Cycle Toolkit, 66
research data, 64
research diary, 46
research methods, 2, 38, 39, 41, 143
research process, 2, 139
research question, 9, 11, 12, 21, 23, 26, 142
research topic. *See* research question
Residual plots, 118

Sage Encyclopedia of Qualitative Research Methods, 39
sample, 83, 86
sample size, 84, 86, 87, 90
sample size calculators, 86
sample size tables, 86
SAS, 63, 97
scholarly, 132
scholarly communication, 133
scholarly journal, 131
scholarship, 10
school data, 64
school district data, 64
school libraries, 5, 10, 15, 133
scientific method, 33
scope, 12, 13, 14, 23, 140
SD. *See* standard deviation
searching, 12
Searching to Learn, 12, 21, 140
secondary data analysis, 47
secondary research, 2
self-selection bias, 90
Shapiro–Wilk test, 101, 116
significance level, 81, 86
simple linear regression, 111, 118
SirsiDynix, 56
Siteimprove, 47, 58
skewed data, 72
snowball sampling, 83
social media, 133
Solomon four-group design, 46
Spearman's correlation coefficient, 109
Springshare, 58
SPSS, 63, 97
stakeholders, 130, 131, 140
standard deviation, 68, 70, 71, 101
standardized estimate, 113, 114
statistical information literacy, 80
statistical literacy, 80

statistical measures, 2
statistical significance, 82, 142
statistical software, 97, 142
statistical tests, 142
statistics, 80, 81, 97, 142
stratified random sampling, 83
Survey Monkey, 64, 87
surveys, 41, 47
synthesis matrix, 28, 29, 30, 140
systematic review, 47

t-tests, 142
test of association, 105, 106, 107
theory-building research, 35
theory-testing research, 35
Tolerance, 116
trade publication, 131, 132
transaction log, 47
transferability, 89, 90

truncation, 19
t-test, 84, 99, 102
Tukey's, 122
Type I error, 81, 86, 142
Type II error, 81, 142

unobtrusive observation, 49
US Census Bureau, 58
Utrecht Data School, 66

variables, 35, 44
VIF, 116

Zotero, 27, 140
η^2, 119

X^2 statistic, 105

ω^2, 119

About the Authors

Caitlin Gerrity is Associate Professor in the Department of Library and Information Science at Southern Utah University.

Scott Lanning is Professor in the Department of Library and Information Science at Southern Utah University.

www.ingramcontent.com/pod-product-compliance
Ingram Content Group UK Ltd.
Pitfield, Milton Keynes, MK11 3LW, UK
UKHW021840220426
470268UK00007B/292